AD Biography
Schoendien Red 1998

Schoendienst, Red. Red : a baseball life
9000818264

D1116732

RED

A Baseball Life

by Red Schoendienst
with Rob Rains

SPORTS PUBLISHING
Champaign, IL 61820

Direction of Production: Susan M. McKinney
Dustjacket and photo insert design: Michelle R. Dressen
Photos: Dave Stradal

ISBN: 1-57167-200-1

SPORTS PUBLISHING
804 N. Neil
Champaign, IL 61820

Printed in the United States.

This book is dedicated to my family,
all of whom have played such a special role in my life—
Mom and Pop, my brothers and sister,
my wife Mary, Mary's Mother and Dad, my kids and my grandkids.
My life has been spent in baseball, but it was a great family that
made everything possible.

CONTENTS

Acknowledgments vi

Foreword *by Stan Musial* vii

1   Dreams Do Come True 1

2   Growing Up 5

3   In the Minors 23

4   A Major Leaguer 37

5   Baseball, and A Family Too 63

6   A Giant, A Brave, and Another World Series 85

7   Fighting a Disease 103

8   Ending One Career, Starting Another 119

9   The Manager 133

10   Hello Mr. Finley 161

11   Whiteyball 175

12   The Hall of Fame 191

13   Coaching Beats Working 201

14   A Great Ride 209

ACKNOWLEDGMENTS

I've got a lot to be grateful about in my life, and my thanks go out to my family and everybody who has helped me along the way.

There were people when I was growing up in Germantown who were there for me. Once I got into baseball, there were my teammates and all the managers and coaches I played for. There were also the fans, and they will never know how important they are for every player, no matter the sport.

It's always good when people see you in a restaurant or someplace and come up and tell you they enjoyed your playing, and tell you it's good to see you and wish you luck in the future.

Several people were helpful in writing this book, and I appreciate their assistance and kind words. My thanks to Peter Bannon and Mike Pearson at Sports Publishing for making this book a reality.

FOREWORD

by Stan Musial

The first time I heard the name Red Schoendienst was in 1945, when I was in the service. I first heard that this kid, Schoendienst, was playing left field for the Cardinals and doing a good job. I guess it caught my attention because that had been my position the previous year.

The next time I heard anything about him, he was playing third base and doing a great job. Then I got word he was playing well at shortstop. I thought, "This kid must be a heck of a player."

Red and I became teammates the following year, and I found out first-hand just out great a player he was.

We soon became more than teammates—being assigned to room together on the road, an arrangement we continued for 10 years, until June 15, 1956, the day Red was traded to the New York Giants.

The rest of us got the word that Red had been traded just as we were boarding a train out of St. Louis for an eastern trip. It was the saddest day of my career. I slammed the door to my train berth shut and didn't open it for a long time.

Red became my opponent for four years, but it didn't spoil our friendship. He went from the Giants to Milwaukee in 1957, and his acquisition made that club great. Most people who were there, including Hank Aaron, don't think the Braves would have won if they had not traded for Red. They needed a second baseman, and they needed a leader. He wasn't ever a rah-rah kind of guy, but he was a leader. He led by example, and he had that innate ability to make those good players around him even better.

Red and I are as close as brothers, and we were reunited when Red rejoined the Cardinals in 1961. We haven't been very far away from each other ever since.

One of Red's traits that I have admired the most over all these years is that he always is on an even keel. He never gets too high or too low. He didn't do it as a player, nor as a manager.

He never complained about anything. He never said anything about his bad eye, or lamented the fact it gave him so much trouble. Even when he was sick, he never told anybody. During all the time he spent in the hospital, recovering from tuberculosis, he never expressed anger or bitterness. I went to see him, and he was suffering. His family wasn't allowed inside the hospital, and he had to wave at his kids through the window to the sidewalk below. He never got upset about it, but concentrated instead on what he needed to do to get well. He then made a great comeback, when most people thought his career was over.

Red would have been a great player no matter what position he played, but second base was his spot. He covered a lot of ground, and he could go back on fly balls to center and right field better than most people I've ever seen. He was a very steady player. He had the greatest hands I've ever seen and he was as good a fundamental player as you ever wanted to see. He almost never made a mistake.

He was a very good manager as well. He was a player's manager, and he again demonstrated the ability to get the most out of his team. When I was the general manager of the Cardinals in 1967 and he was the manager, we didn't make many roster moves the entire season and we won the World Series. The players enjoyed Red and they respected him.

Red loves baseball, and he has dedicated his live to the game. He has earned the respect of everybody he has come into contact with over the 53 years he has worn a major-league uniform. He has earned his proper place in the Hall of Fame in Cooperstown.

Baseball is different today than it was when Red and I played, but it's amazing in the game how the years run together. Red and I played with players who played in the 1930s, and we played in the 1940s, 1950s and 1960s. We played against guys who played in the 1970s, so it's hard to say one era is better than another. I have always believed, however, that the great players from any era would have been great no matter when they played, and I put Red in that category.

Red and I had more time to enjoy ourselves when we played than do today's players. Society is so much faster paced today. We traveled by train, and we had time to socialize. We had time to go out to dinner and the theater, and had more leisure time. We got to go a lot of places and meet a lot of famous people, both in the game of baseball and in the entertainment world, politics and business.

We always enjoyed going to New York, and we spent many evenings with Horace Stoneham, the owner of the Giants. We hung out at Toots Shor's restaurant, and all the famous people came there to see what other celebrities were there.

We were in New York one time when I got a call from Ty Cobb, wanting Red and I to go to breakfast with him. Ty noticed me putting cream and sugar in my coffee, and he said, "Both of those aren't good for you. You should cut out one of them." I said OK, and since that day I've never put cream in my coffee.

Cobb asked me how old I was, and I answered 35, and he asked me if I intended to play a few more years. I said I did, and he told me, "You should start drinking wine at dinner. It's good for your digestion." I started drinking wine, and I played seven more years. Red just sat there quietly, taking it all in and never saying a word. He played until he was 40 as well.

I've learned a lot from Red over the years. He taught me how to hunt. One day he invited me to go quail hunting, and he told me to wear my old clothes. I showed up at his house wearing a sport coat. I didn't have any old clothes. That was the first time I ever went hunting, but Red was patient and taught me well. We went out a lot after that, hunting for quail and ducks, and we also spent a lot of time sitting in a boat, fishing, or enjoying the beauty of a golf course.

Red loves the outdoors, almost as much as he loves baseball and his family. Just as our lives have been entwined over the years, our families' have become one as well. Our wives, Lil and Mary, became lifelong friends. All of our kids grew up together and remain close. We really are one, big happy family.

A lot of guys had the privilege of playing with or for Red over the years, and I'm proud I was one of them. He is one of the kindest, most decent men I've ever known in my life. Even more important than having been his teammate or roommate, however, is having been his friend for so many years. They don't come any better.

Chapter 1

DREAMS DO COME TRUE

When I reported to the Cardinals' war-time spring training camp in Cairo, Illinois, in March of 1945, I was 22 years old and more than a little uncertain about what I was doing.

I thought I could play baseball, but whether I could play it well enough to succeed in the major leagues remained to be seen. I was nervous, excited and a little scared all at the same time, a jumbled mixture of emotions.

Making the team and starting in left field on opening day in Chicago was one of the greatest thrills in my life, but I didn't know then how many more special moments were going to come my way.

The 1998 season will mark the 54th consecutive year I've been privileged to wear a major-league uniform, and in a lot of ways, the season doesn't seem that far removed from 1945, when floods forced us to move spring training back to St. Louis.

In between there have been a lot of highs, a few lows, a lot of laughs, a lot of smiles, and some tears. I was hired, fired and traded. I came down with tuberculosis, but didn't let it get me down. I married a wonderful woman, and together we had four terrific kids and have celebrated 50 years together.

My life has been a great ride, in and out of baseball. So many people have helped me achieve my boyhood dreams, and some might not even realize how much they have meant to me over the years.

There were so many defining moments that, even though I perhaps didn't realize it at the time, impacted the course of my life.

What if, after an errant staple struck me in the left eye as a 16-year-old working in a Civilian Conservation Corps camp, doctors had gone ahead and removed the eye, not listening to my pleas to do everything they could to save it?

What if Joe Linneman and I had not decided to hitchhike to St. Louis to attend a Cardinals' tryout camp in 1942? One of the scouts, Walter Shannon, told me later somebody would have found me anyway, that I was destined to play in the major leagues, but you never know.

What if Mary, my future wife, had not bumped into me on a streetcar following a game in 1945? She would have found me another way —she was after me.

What if I hadn't been suffering from the effects of tuberculosis, always leaving me tired and rundown, for several years before doctors actually found out what was wrong?

What if I had decided to sign with Fred Haney and the expansion Los Angeles Angels before the 1961 season instead of coming back to the Cardinals to end my career?

What if Johnny Keane had not resigned after the 1964 World Series, opening the manager's job at a time the public relations fallout of hiring an outsider might have been disastrous for the ballclub?

What if I had not come back to coach for the Cardinals in 1979, choosing instead to pursue managing jobs in other cities?

If even one of those events had produced a different result, my life would have turned out differently. There are near misses in everyone's lives, but you rarely take the time to think back about what might have been.

I might not have ever reached the major leagues and wouldn't have played, coached or managed in nine World Series. I might not have played in 10 All-Star games, managed two and coached in others. I might not have managed the Cardinals for 12 years, longer than anyone else in history.

I might not have been inducted into the Hall of Fame, or played with some of the immortals in baseball history like Stan Musial, Hank Aaron, Willie Mays and Warren Spahn.

I might not have managed other greats who made their way to Cooperstown like Bob Gibson and Lou Brock, or been around to coach a future Hall of Famer, Ozzie Smith, or work for a manager who should make it there, Whitey Herzog.

Mom and Pop would be amazed by everything that has happened in my life, and how our country has changed so much since the days of the Depression, when Pop always was working somewhere and going hunting to make certain we had something to eat.

My life has been an incredible ride, and when I think back on the places I've been, the people I've met and the great times I've enjoyed along the way, it seems like a dream. I guess dreams, or at least the ones of a boy growing up in the small town of Germantown, Illinois, can come true.

Chapter 2

GROWING UP

As far back as I can remember, baseball was one of the most important parts of my life. The joke among the people in Germantown was that if you needed to find Al—everybody in my family had red hair, so we were all known by our real name or another nickname—you only had to look in two places, the baseball field or the river. I was certain to be one place or the other, playing baseball or fishing.

My mom and dad knew how much I loved baseball, and they tried to encourage me as much as possible. They also knew I didn't care much for school, and they tried to push me in that direction as well, but without much success. My dad, Joe, had been a pretty good catcher when he was young in the Clinton County league, and when he got older, he became an umpire. I never saw anyone dispute one of his calls.

My mom, Mary, used to stitch up baseballs for me, my brothers and friends like Joe Linneman to use. They were made of sawdust in the middle, then had a cover stitched over the top. They used to last about three or four swings, but that was all we had. If we didn't have any of those balls, we would take a hickory nut or a corncob or a rock or some string we found, maybe from an old baseball, get the cover stitched over it and use that until it fell apart. Bats were easier to find. All you had to do was get a piece of wood and store it some place where it could dry out real well. Then you had a bat.

One Christmas morning, mom and dad and all seven kids—six boys and a girl—trudged through the snow to church, then came home to see what presents were wrapped under the tree. We found a glove and a sawdust ball. It didn't make any difference that there probably was a foot of snow on the ground outside. We all charged out the door and put that ball, glove and a bat to use. The ball probably lasted about three or four swings before we knocked the cover off it. We broke the bat, and ripped the lining out of the glove. We left everything laying in the snow, but we considered that a pretty good Christmas.

I was about six years old then, in 1929, and it was right at the beginning of the Depression. As kids growing up, we didn't know times were that tough. Everyone had a garden, Pop was always working whenever and wherever he could, and he would go hunting for rabbits or squirrels to bring us something home to eat. We didn't have indoor plumbing or electricity, but nobody else did either, so we didn't feel deprived of anything. I never went to bed hungry. I was about 10 when Pop hooked up the electricity into our house. We had used coal oil lanterns before that.

Looking back on it, I can understand and appreciate how hard it was for my mom and dad to keep the family going during those times. We didn't know anything about their worries, and that's the way it should be. We were just kids; we never thought about not having a roof over our heads or food to eat. We just managed somehow, getting food out of the garden, eating the game Pop shot for dinner. Everybody had fruit trees, and mom made certain we canned enough fruits and vegetables from the garden to get us through the winter. We got water out of the well, and had to be sure we carried in enough to run the stove and to give everybody a bath. Mom used to heat the water on the stove in a big, old black pot. On Sundays you had to drag in enough water that she could do the wash on Monday. It's hard to believe that those were the so-called "good ol' days," but we survived. We didn't know any better. Kids today would have a fit if you asked them to do all of the chores we had to do.

Not that we didn't complain sometimes. I'm certain there were many times when I was chopping wood, carrying water or working in the garden when I would rather have been fishing or playing baseball. Parents back then weren't afraid to swat their kids when they misbehaved, however, and Pop even had a rather unique tool that he used to punish us when we acted up or didn't do what we were told. Pop was a big man, about 6-foot-1, and he was strong as an ox from all the work he did. He was always the security guy around town because nobody ever challenged him. We were his own kids, and we should have known better, too.

Everybody wore those big old bib overalls, and we had a large nail hanging on a wall out on the front porch. If you talked back to mom or disagreed with something she said, or for any other reason that Pop thought was wrong, he would just pick you up with one hand and hang you up on that nail. You would just hang there swinging, about two feet off the ground. He never said a word to you, If you said something, you stayed up there longer. After a while, he'd come by and pick you up and set you down. No words, nothing. You learned not to get out of line, because he would just leave you there, hanging. Parents couldn't get away with that today. The kids would either sue them or somebody would file charges of child abuse.

My parents probably would have been pleased if I had cared more for school, but I just never did. Some of my friends didn't much like it either, and if we ran into each other walking to school and the fish were biting, well, we never made it to school that day. When Pop found out about it, that's when you really stayed up on that nail.

If you weren't at school, they had people who went out looking for you. It was a small town. There weren't any telephones, but they knew where to look. When they caught you, they brought you back to school and then you had to do extra things like stay after school and write your name on the blackboard a hundred times or so. I had a long name, too. No matter whether it was in school or at home, you were always disciplined when you did something you shouldn't do, or didn't do something you were supposed to do. People don't discipline their kids enough these days. It may have been rough, but it taught you a lesson and made you think about what you were doing.

Summer was always the best time of the year, because once your chores were done, you could play baseball or fish all day and not have to be stuck in school. It didn't matter how many kids were out, you just played some kind of game. We played one game where we would stand in the front yard, throw the ball over the house, run around to the back yard and try to catch it before it came down. Mom and dad didn't care for that game much because sometimes the ball landed on the roof. When you didn't have anyone to play catch with, you threw the ball against the side of the house and bounced it to yourself, but they usually yelled at you for that and you had to find something else to do.

Kids today don't know all of the creative games you can play in baseball. They think you have to have nine kids, wear uniforms and play in an organized league somewhere. We played with hickory nuts and broomsticks and bottle caps. We played pepper. We just played. Nobody ever had to entertain us or find something for us to do. You don't see kids doing that today, and that's a shame.

The year of the baseball strike, 1994, my brother Elmer and I were driving around and it struck both of us how we didn't see any kids out playing baseball. There were all of these fields at the schools, and they were just sitting there, empty. You used to see kids out there, playing sandlot games. We didn't see anybody, and it was shocking. Kids today don't get outside and play enough, unless it's in an organized league somewhere. They have too many other things to do, like Nintendo, and computers and watching television. We didn't have television. You even have a hard time today getting somebody to go fishing with you, much less go out and play baseball.

It might have been different growing up in a big city like St. Louis, but Germantown was a small town. The population was only about 800 people, and we could walk every place. It was about a mile or so to the Shoal Creek, where we usually went fishing or swimming. The Kaskaskia River was a little farther away, but we went there sometimes. The school was about four blocks away, a much shorter walk, but for some reason, it was a lot harder to walk in that direction.

When Red was being honored a few years ago in Germantown, we drove over and we drove around and around and couldn't find the school. Red tried to say it was because it was a new school, but I teased him that it was no wonder he didn't do anything in school because he couldn't find it.

—*Mary Schoendienst*

The roads were pretty bad, and Pop and a lot of the other men in town worked in the coal mines in Breese, which was about four miles away. They went by horse and buggy, and they had to get up at 3 a.m. so they would be able to start work at 7 a.m. They didn't get back home until 8 or 9 p.m. There also was a mine in New Baden where Pop worked sometimes. It was eight miles away, but they had a whistle you could hear all the way to Germantown. They used to blow that whistle at 3 o'clock in the afternoon to let people know whether they should show up for work the next day or not. Mom used to always tell us to make certain we were outside at 3 p.m. so we could listen for the whistle to find out if Pop was working the next day or not.

We never had a car, and nobody we knew had one, either. We didn't have a bicycle, and we were lucky to have a coaster wagon. One of my brothers, Julius, decided one time to try to make a bicycle so we all went to the junk yard and found all the pieces that we thought it would take to put a bicycle together. He put it together and it ran, but that was about it. I can still close my eyes and see him riding that bicycle down the street, looking all high and mighty. It didn't have any front roller bearings, though, it was just running on the axle. The next thing we knew, the front wheel broke off and Julius was flying over the handlebars and soaring through the air. That's how fast he had been going. It still breaks me up today to think about him going through the air like that. He was lucky he wasn't hurt, but kids back then didn't seem to get hurt from stuff like that. He got skinned up, but that was about it. I can still picture him walking back up the street, carrying part of the bike in each hand.

He was a rough kid. Everybody had a nickname back then, and his was Bud. People got their nicknames out of the comic strips or just from somebody about their physical appearance, like their hair or something like that. My oldest brother, Andy, was nicknamed Ducks. Eugene, next in line, was called Mickey. When I was about six or seven years old, I was in a play at school where I played a character named Rex the King. There are still some oldtimers from Germantown who call me Rex when they run into me or see me at the ballpark. My younger brothers were Elmer and Joey. My sister's name was Loretta. She was the second oldest, next to Andy. Even our parents called us by our nicknames, unless we were in trouble. Then they called us by our real names.

When I was growing up, Andy had a job driving for a doctor in town, Doctor Myers, in his old Model T Ford. He would have to get up at 4 a.m. so he could drive the doctor into all of the small towns around Germantown if somebody was having a baby. All of my brothers worked at various jobs, either in town or out on the farms. We used to go out and shuck corn, and we would have to do it until our hands started to bleed. Nobody complained; it was our way of helping out the family.

I don't remember Andy playing much baseball, but all of my brothers played and three of them—Julius, Elmer and Joey—played in the minor leagues. Julius made it all the way to Triple A with the Cardinals, in Columbus, before he quit when he got sent down to a lower level. Elmer was a good player, but his career was shortened by a bus accident when he was playing in Duluth, Minnesota. Several of his teammates were killed, and Elmer hurt his back. A year later, his career was over. Joey made it up to Class B before he hung it up.

Whenever there was a big event like a heavyweight fight or something, all of us would go over to my grandma's house to listen to it on the radio. It was one of those big old console radios, and all the kids would lay down on the floor and listen. The kids never got to pick what programs we listened to—it was always the grownups who made those decisions. It was fun listening to guys like Franc Laux and Ray Schmidt.

Most ballgames weren't broadcast on the radio back then. We all followed either the Cardinals or Browns—I was a Cardinals fan—and we got the results by going by the ice cream parlor after school, where they had a ticker or something, or by waiting to read the story in the St. Louis newspaper the next day.

The newspapers used to be dropped off in bundles at the train station, and they cost 2 cents each. My brother used to deliver the *Globe-Democrat*, and I would go along a lot of the time to help him out. The train wouldn't stop as it came through Germantown; the porter would just throw the bundle of newspapers off on the loading dock. We would pick them up, then walk around town delivering them.

It was hard to know a lot about the players back then, because you never got to see them play and only knew what you read about them in the newspaper. Nobody even thought about going to St. Louis for a game. That was 40 miles away, and people just didn't do that. Fans today have so much more knowledge and information about all of the players, they seem much more familiar to them. A lot more people go to the games, even from small towns far away from the team's home city, and those who don't go to the games still watch them on television. I wouldn't have known Joe Medwick or Frankie Frisch or any of the other members of the Gas House Gang unless I recognized them from their pictures in the newspaper. We idolized those players more back then than kids do today, because we didn't know so much about them. In many cases today, we know too much about a player. I know there are a lot of modern-day players who wish they could be as anonymous as the players in the 1930s were, but they have to realize they wouldn't be getting the big paychecks now either if that was the case. You've got to take the bad with the good, and for most players, the media and fan attention is the price they have to pay for being a highly paid star.

A man named Jack Fruit ran a garage in Germantown, and he had a radio and was a big baseball fan. We went there to listen sometimes whenever a big event was on, and I remember trying to listen to the broadcast of the first night game from Cincinnati. It was tough, because the radio was cutting in and out. You would hear that a batter had two strikes, and then the radio would cut out and not come back in for five minutes. By then somebody else was batting and you had to try to figure out what had happened.

I was always more into playing myself than following the major leaguers and worrying about what they were doing. I was fortunate to have a lot of brothers and a lot of friends like Joe Linneman so we were always able to get up a game. It's funny how Joe and I have remained such good friends our entire lives. We grew up three blocks away from each other, with all of the same interests, and now we are business partners, still live close together and see each other all the time. Joe didn't make it in baseball, even though he played in the minors for a while, but he became a very successful businessman.

My older brothers played on some of the teams around Germantown, and that's how I got started in organized baseball too. One of the men in town, Ed Roach, was in charge of the Clinton County league and he did a great job of keeping things organized and making certain all of the small towns around Germantown had their own team. He was the manager of the Germantown team, and he knew baseball. He helped give me the knowledge of the fundamentals of baseball that I used to make it to the major leagues.

There were some pretty good players in that league. The men would work all week and play on Sunday. It was always a town team, like Germantown, Breese, New Baden, Albers, etc. so there was always a lot of pride in wanting to win for your town. They were exciting games. My dad was the umpire back then, and he was definitely in charge. He'd talk to you, about baseball and other stuff, and people always listened to him.

I listened to Ed Roach a lot too. He was a disciplinarian, and he understood the game. He was really keen on fundamentals, and that's where I learned a lot of my early lessons in what to do on the field. He was always telling us how important it was to think when we were on the field, to know where the baserunners were and how many outs there were. He always made certain we knew what inning it was and what the score was. It's amazing now that so many players, even in the major leagues, don't realize how important it is to know all those things if your team is going to win. They either throw to the wrong base, forget how many outs there are, or make a different mental mistake. Ed Roach would have thrown a tantrum at some of the fundamental mistakes I've seen major leaguers make over the years.

Part of the reason I think fundamentals came easier for me is that I just loved to play the game so much. I played every chance I got, I wanted to get better, and so I listened when people offered advice and constructive criticism. Some skills I think I was born with, but others developed over the years simply because of hard work and practice.

When I was growing up, not many people went to college and if people stuck it out through high school that was considered a lot of schooling. I had too many other interests, however, and when I turned 16 and had the chance, the first thing I did was work up the nerve to ask my mom and dad if I could quit school.

They didn't want me to quit, but they knew I was cutting classes almost as often as I was going by then anyway. They asked what I planned to do if I quit school, and I had my answer ready—I was going to get a job in the Civilian Conservation Corps, the CCC.

The CCC had been started by the government as a way to help people get jobs during the Depression. You mostly did projects that needed to be done anyway, like working on roads and highways and building fences, so it was probably one of the most worthwhile government programs ever created.

My brothers, Mickey and Eugene, already were in the CCC. Mickey was assigned to a unit in California, and most of their time was spent fighting forest fires. When I turned 16, I got my Social Security card, quit school and Steve Kohnen, another childhood friend of mine, Linneman and I all signed up. We had been working on farms, and one day Steve and I were just sitting around, talking. I had a half dollar—I don't know where I got it from—but I told Steve, "I've been thinking about going into the CCC camp. It's got to be easier than what we're doing." Working on those farms, you had to get up at 4 a.m. to get there and you didn't get home until 10 p.m., and the next day you had to do it all over again. Steve said that sounded like a good idea to him.

I pulled the half dollar coin out of my pants pocket, and told Steve, "If this coin falls heads, we're going to sign up on Monday for the CCC camp." It fell heads, and we went and signed up for six months.

We were all assigned to the camp in Greenville, Illinois, about 30 miles from Germantown, but still a long way away in those days. The roads were bad, and it was hard to get from one town to the other. There was no regular transportation between the two towns, so we must have hitchhiked to get there. It was just like the Army when we arrived. We had to stand in lines to be issued our uniforms, which were like fatigues, and everybody was assigned to a barracks. There were about 50 guys in each barracks.

The jobs paid a dollar a day. You kept $5 and the remaining $25 was sent home. I guess they didn't want us losing it all in the card games and craps games that always seemed to be going on. I stood around and watched, and usually guys would end up trying to borrow money. If I knew the guy and thought he would pay me back, I'd give it to him. With interest payments, I wound up making a little more money than my $5 a month.

One time a guy owed me $6 and wouldn't pay. I got hold of the supply sergeant, and found out he was gone. The sergeant had taken his locker, and confiscated all of his belongings. I found a way to get in there, and was surprised to discover the guy wore the same size shoes as my dad. I don't know if my dad ever knew where his new shoes came from.

The only difference that I saw between the CCC and the Army was you didn't have to fight. The officers still told you what to do, and the discipline was very strict. You had to wear a dress uniform every night for inspection. The officers in charge were big on cleanliness and making certain everything was in order, just like the Army. We had to line up for roll call every morning before breakfast, salute the flag, and then everybody separated to do their individual jobs. Some people planted trees, others painted bridges or worked on dams, built fences or worked on building and improving the roads.

The thing that appealed most to me about the camps was that each camp had its own baseball team, much like the town teams in Germantown and the other small towns in the area. We played after work and on weekends, and there were some pretty good players on those teams.

One of Red's older brothers had been playing on the CCC team and he signed a contract with the Cardinals and went off to play ball. The manager of the ball team got up and said, "If anybody thinks they can make the team, come out to practice." Red was in another barracks, and when I told him that, he said, "Let's try to make that team."

I said, "Are you kidding? The guys on that team are 21, 22 and 23 years old. We're 16." He said we would at least get a ride out to the lake, which was a couple of miles away, and we could go swimming. We went, and the manager told us if we wanted to play to be back Sunday at 1:30. I said, "I don't think I can make that. I need to go home and see my mom."

We went to Germantown for the weekend, then got together and decided to come back for the game. Red played shortstop and I pitched, and we finished the year with the team. I ended up winning 17 games and losing one.

— Joe Linneman

Each CCC camp also had its own boxing team. It was another way to keep the guys occupied so they didn't have much free time. I thought about boxing, but they used those big, old 16-ounce gloves. You could hit pretty good with those things, but you didn't want to get hit by them. I fooled around with it a little bit, but I never got serious about it.

Tuesday nights were the nights when everybody got to leave camp and go into town. There was a restaurant in Greenville called the "Dynomite" and the lady that ran it gave all of the CCC guys a break, selling them a malt and a hamburger for 20 cents. That was a real treat. There also was a theater in town that cost a dime, and that usually was our big night out.

When we weren't playing baseball or out on the town,
we were working. One day Red and I were building fences
down on a slope. We would stretch the wire as tight as we
could get it, and then use a hammer to drive a staple into
a dry hedgepost, which was almost as hard as a piece of
steel.

Red called me over and said, "Help me hold this wire."
I hit the nail, but it glanced off the post and ricochetted
into Red's eye.

— *Joe Linneman*

It was the most intense pain I've ever felt in my life. I knew exactly what had happened, but I didn't know how bad it was. I just prayed I wasn't going to lose my eye, which I knew would end my days of playing baseball.

They loaded me in a truck and drove me to the Marine hospital in St. Louis, which is now St. Joseph's Hospital in Kirkwood. The doctors began to examine my eye, and took me to see more doctors at another hospital. I was in the hospital for five weeks, being examined by different specialists. Everybody seemed to agree that I was going to lose the eye, that the doctors would have to remove it. If that had indeed happened, there would have been no way I could have seen well enough to ever hit a baseball again.

I protested, as strongly and sternly as possible, for the doctors to save the eye. I explained that I was a baseball player, and they couldn't jeopardize my future without at least trying to see if it could be saved. In the meantime my mom had come in from Germantown, and she was there with me while the doctors tried to decide what to do.

Finally one doctor agreed that the eye could be saved. That didn't mean I was well, however. I had to begin some intense treatments, because I was experiencing double vision and spots. The accident had left me with about 20/200 vision in that eye, and I really didn't know how it was going to affect me when I went back to playing baseball again.

I had one previous scare with my eye, and it had turned out all right. When I was about 12, my brothers and I were taking apart some old junk cars and I was using an old jack to crank up a car and the handle slipped and came up and hit me in the face, just an inch or so below my left eye. It broke a bone, but luckily didn't affect my vision.

Before I could really worry about how well I would be able to see a baseball, I had two more months of service to complete in the CCC. World War II had broken out, and people were signing up for the Army or getting drafted, and the CCC was disbanded. My brothers, Andy and Mickey, both signed up and went, but I didn't want to go. I took a job as a supply clerk at Scott Field in Belleville, played baseball and waited for the Army to come calling on me.

The eye still bothered me, and I was still required to do eye exercises everyday to try to restore as much vision as possible. It didn't bother me as much as I had expected on the baseball field, although there were some days I really had trouble seeing and picking up the ball from the pitcher, especially when it was cloudy. Those days I was glad I wasn't facing a wild guy throwing 100 mph, or it could have been really scary.

My eyesight came back enough for me to still believe I had a future in baseball, and when Joe Linneman and I read in the newspaper that the Cardinals were going to hold a tryout camp, we decided we should go and give it a shot. Joe was a pitcher on the Germantown team, and he was pretty good, but really I don't think either one of us went to that tryout camp thinking we had it made.

The Cardinals were playing the Brooklyn Dodgers that week, and the announcement had said that anyone attending the tryout camp would be allowed to stay and watch the game for free. That convinced us we should go, since neither of us had ever seen a major league game.

Over the years, the popularized version of the story has been that Joe and I were playing pool one night when we heard about the tryout camp over the radio and decided we should go. That's partially true—we were playing pool and they did talk about the tryout camp on the radio—but we had already read about it in the newspaper and made up our minds to go. Another friend of ours from Germantown decided to go with us as well.

One question we hadn't answered was how we were going to get to St. Louis, 40 miles away, since neither of us had a car. We ended up hitchhiking on a Pevely Dairy truck into St. Louis. That got us as far as the corner of Grand and Chouteau, and then we walked the rest of the way to Sportsman's Park, about a mile and a half.

We weren't prepared for what happened when we got to the park, and I don't think the Cardinals were ready for it either. A total of 398 kids showed up for the tryout, not exactly a manageable number for the scouts to be able to get an accurate reading on whether a kid could hit, pitch, field, throw and run.

The first thing they did was split the kids into two groups. Those who lived in St. Louis were sent home and told to come back the next day. Those of us who were from out of town stayed to work out.

They pinned a number on the back of everyone's shirts, then sent the would-be players through all of the different facets of the game. I took groundballs at shortstop, then moved to third, then they told me to switch to second, so I played there for a while. We also had to show the scouts how well we could run. That seemed to be the two skills they were most interested in, and I must have showed them something they liked because a lot of the kids were sent home that night, but they asked me—and Joe—to come back the next day.

Joe's aunt lived in Kirkwood, and he was going to stay at her house. He invited me to go with him, but I told him I had someplace else to stay. He left, and then I asked myself, "Where are you going to spend the night?" I didn't have a place to stay, I was just too proud to tell Joe that I didn't have anyplace to go.

The problem was complicated by the fact I had a quarter to my name. That was all of the money I had. I walked down the street, and came up to a little restaurant. I went in, sat down at the counter and ordered a hot dog— it probably cost a dime—and the lady running the place asked if I wanted something to drink. I said water was fine, but she gave me a glass of milk and said, "I won't charge you for that." By looking at me she probably could tell I didn't have much money.

I was sitting on the stool eating the hot dog when she asked me if I was trying out for the Cardinals. After hearing me answer yes, she said, "You look like a nice young man. You know something? You might be a big league ballplayer some day." I wonder how she knew that.

Leaving the restaurant, I felt a little better but still had no idea where I was going to spend the night. I wandered into Union Station, the big train station, and thought maybe I could lay down on one of the benches. Before I could get settled, however, a security guard came by and told me to leave —only people coming and going on a train were allowed to stay there. I went back outside, and went across the street to a park. I sat down on a bench, and decided it probably was the best place I was going to find even though it was hard as a rock. I tried to get as comfortable as I could, and probably because I was so tired, drifted off to sleep. Don't try that today, or you might not wake up in the morning.

In the middle of the night, it started raining—hard. I tried to get back inside Union Station, but the security guard wouldn't let me in. I finally found an old flea bag hotel, and went in just to get out of the rain. A room was 15 cents, so I gave the clerk all the money I had left and went up to the room. I was so tired, I didn't pay attention to the room or the bed but just laid down and quickly went to sleep.

In the morning, I was covered with bites from some kind of bugs. I was really ate up. When I got to the ballpark, they gave me some lotion to put on the bites, but I think that was part of the reason I moved so fast that day. I made up my mind I was going to swallow my pride and stay with Joe's aunt the next night, and I did.

One thing I didn't have was money, and I was hungry. I asked one of the scouts if they were going to give us something to eat, and he told me to go see a woman in the Cardinals' office. It was Mary Murphy, who was the secretary to the team's owner, Sam Breadon. She was a wonderful lady and turned into a good friend. On that day, however, all she saw in me was a hungry, tired kid and she took pity on me. She asked me how I was going to get home without any money, and I said I would walk. She said, "Well you still have to have something to eat." She gave me a quarter so I could go back to that little restaurant and get something to eat. We worked out all day, then went to Joe's aunt's house. The only problem was he had forgotten his equipment, so I crawled under a big iron gate at the ballpark, got the attention of a security guard and went in and got all his stuff.

The camp continued for the rest of the week, and I know the scouts must have thought I had some ability because they never told me to leave. There were some other quality kids in that camp too, including two who would go on to become pretty fair major leaguers—two catchers who were buddies from The Hill in St. Louis, Joe Garagiola and Yogi Berra.

Branch Rickey was still the general manager of the Cardinals at that time, and late in the week I remember he took the three of us in his big black Lincoln over to Forest Park to work out, because there wasn't enough room at the ballpark. I remember two things about that experience, that he was a terrible driver and throwing batting practice to Garagiola and Berra. That car ride was scary. He was talking and driving like there was nobody else on the road. There wasn't too many people on the road, which was a good thing.

I'm certain Joe and Yogi must have thrown to me too, but for some reason I don't remember any of the details. I thought I had a good week, but the camp ended and none of the scouts said anything about offering me a contract. I hitchhiked back home, very disappointed. I didn't even get to stay for the Cardinals-Dodgers game.

As it turned out, Joe Mathes, the head Cardinals' scout, had only been around for the first part of the week before he had to leave town. When he came back, he asked the other scouts which players had been signed. "What happened to that skinny freckle-faced kid, did you sign him up?" Mathes asked. Told the answer was no, Mathes got upset. He had somebody get in touch with me in Germantown, and I was told to come back over to St. Louis to report to the ballpark.

I hitched another ride on the milk truck, walked to the stadium, and found out the Cardinals wanted to sign me. The major-league team was working out on the field, preparing for a game, and the scouts sent me out to shag flies in the outfield, then it came my turn to hit.

One of the coaches told me each of the extra players got five pitches, but I didn't know he meant just that, not swings. I took two pitches because neither were strikes, then I swung at the next two. I took the fifth pitch, then all I heard was the other players yelling for me to get the hell out of there. I scooted out of there as quickly as I could.

Unfortunately, I wasn't old enough to sign the contract by myself— my dad had to sign. I got my signing bonus anyway, a ham sandwich and a glass of milk—and was sent back home to get ready to leave for the minor leagues the next day. I didn't have much to pack except my glove.

Mathes and another Cardinals' executive, Bill Walsingham, drove over to Germantown to get my dad's signature on the contract. They found Pop up on a ladder, painting the bridge of the new 161 highway that was coming through town. They yelled up to him, and he asked who they were and what they wanted. When he got the answer, he climbed down the ladder, wiped his hands on his overalls, and signed the contract giving me permission to join the Cardinals.

"Give him a chance. He can play," Pop said.

A chance was all I was looking for. The next morning I boarded a bus in Breese, Illinois, on my way to Bowling Green, Kentucky, where I was to join the Union City, Tennessee farm team in the Class D Kitty League. The Cardinals were going to pay me $75 a month to play baseball. I didn't think life could get any better than that.

Chapter 3

IN THE MINORS

It probably was a negative way to look at it, but riding that bus from Breese to Bowling Green, Kentucky, gave me a lot of time to think about what I was getting myself into. What if I didn't make it? What would I do then?

I was willing to give it some time, three years or so, and see what kind of progress I had made. If I was lucky, I was hoping I would advance from Class D to Class B baseball by then, moving up the ladder a level at a time. There were a lot more minor league teams in those days, and it was not unusual for players to spend a long time in the minors before ever being considered for a spot on the major-league roster.

If those three years went by and I was still in Class D or even Class C, that would be the evidence indicating to me that I probably was not much of a prospect and needed to find something else to do. As much as I disliked school when I was younger, I knew my only choice would be to go back to school and learn a trade.

Luckily, three years later, I was in the majors and didn't ever have to worry about learning any other trade or pursuing any other type of job.

If I had been forced to make a prediction about my future after my first game in the minors, however, it might have been a far different story.

Everett Johnson was the manager of Union City, and it wasn't a good team. When I joined the team on the road in Bowling Green, I didn't know there was a good chance the team was about to be shut down. Nobody was coming to the home games, and the front office people had told Branch Rickey in St. Louis that if the organization didn't come up with better players and the team could start winning, they were going to go out of business. Other teams in the league also were in financial trouble, and after I had played only six games, the entire league shut down.

My first game as a professional was a good night offensively as I got four hits. My offensive efforts were overshadowed, however, by what happened when we were in the field in the ninth inning. I was playing second base, and a grounder went through my legs for an error. The rightfielder and centerfielder both came in to try to pick it up, and collided in a heap. One of them picked it up and threw it back to me. The runner who had been on first when the play began was trying to score, and I uncorked a wild throw to the plate. That was my second error on the play. He scored, and we lost the game.

I was slumped down in front of my locker after the game, feeling sorry for myself, when Johnson walked up to me and said, "Mr. Rickey was here tonight and he would like to talk to you." I honestly thought my career was going to end just as it was beginning; that he was going to say the scouts had make a mistake and was going to release me on the spot. So much for my three-year plan. Of all the games in the Cardinals' minor-league system that he could have attended, why had he happened to pick this one? What rotten luck.

When Rickey came up to my locker, however, I found out he was just trying to comfort an unsure, 19-year-old rookie.

"Young man," he started out. "Let me tell you something. This is your first time away from home. You signed your first contract, and you played your first game. That would make anybody nervous."

I said, "Yes sir."

"You made a couple of errors tonight," he said. "Yes sir," I said again.

Rickey continued. "You're a fine ballplayer. But let me tell you something. You're going to make a few more errors before you get out of this game. You look like you could be a pretty good ballplayer. Go out and get them tomorrow."

That conversation allowed me to sleep a little easier that night.

I collected more hits in my second game, actually going eight-for-eight to begin my professional career, before I went to my manager and surprised him by asking him if it was OK if I batted lefthanded when there was a righthander pitcher. I never will forget the look on his face. He thought I was crazy—until I explained why I wanted to do it, that I couldn't pick up the curve from a righthander without turning my head because of my problems with my left eye. He still was a little skeptical, but he said if I wanted to try it I could.

When the Kitty League disbanded, I didn't know what was going to happen to me. Some players were released and sent home, others were shipped off to join other farm teams all over the country. My next destination was Albany, Georgia.

It was the farthest I had ever been away from home, but I was glad to be playing baseball and I was determined to do the best job I could and enjoy it for as long as it lasted. Albany was a nice little town, and we played in an old ballpark that had a lot of character. It helped that Joe Linneman and I were together, making the transition of being so far away from home a lot easier.

There was one thing Joe and I noticed immediately about that ballpark—you weren't going to hit a home run to centerfield, I don't care how strong you were. The field was laid out so it was below ground level, and there was a big hill going right down the rightfield foul line. I think it was 360 feet down both foul lines. There was a slope in centerfield, where the scoreboard was. Nobody hit it up that slope, not even some of the great players who came through Albany during their careers, like Johnny Mize.

I hit a home run—almost—inside the park one day. It was a line drive that went between the leftfielder and the centerfielder. The centerfielder had tried to make a shoestring catch but had missed, and the ball rolled behind him and up the hill. I circled the bases, but the umpire ruled I missed third base and called me out. That meant I was only credited with a double. I really think I touched third, but there was no way I was going to win the argument—

probably the first time I had that lesson taught to me. Whatever the umpire said was all that mattered.

Defensively, I had my troubles at Albany. Those errors I had made for Union City had been the start of a bad stretch. I finished the year at Albany with 27 errors in only 68 games, and I can't blame the ballpark. It was one of the best I ever played in.

There were some neat people whom I met while playing in Albany. One was a man who some of the players nicknamed Bad Eye. He was an older black gentleman who worked as the groundskeeper on the field. He was called Bad Eye because he was only able to see out of one eye. Bad Eye had an uncanny ability to tell you whether it was going to rain or not. He would be out there working on the field before the game and he would say, "Well, I don't think we're going to get this game in." There wouldn't be a cloud in the sky or any threat of rain, and he would say, "It's going to rain in the fourth." And by God if it didn't start raining in the fourth inning and they had to call the game. I don't know how he did it.

Several years later after I was in the majors, the Cardinals traveled through Georgia on their way north to open the season and stopped to play a game in Albany. Bad Eye had retired, but he still came to the game and came by to say hello. Those are the kinds of friendships that are really special, because he was such a good guy and worked so hard at his job and cared so much that he was doing a good job.

Another special person in Albany was the lady whom a lot of the players boarded with. None of us ever had any money—we weren't making much to begin with and I was always trying to send some home—and that lady really took care of us. I saw her on the same barnstorming trip north, and thanked her for putting up with me and my teammates.

Three of us stayed together in a real small room. Red and I slept together in a double bed and Jack Burchard slept along the wall. We tried to stay asleep until 12:30 or so after night games so we wouldn't have to eat breakfast. We were only making $75 a month. Then we had a pear and a Coca-Cola on our way downtown.

— Joe Linneman

There was a little restaurant where the ballclub had a prearranged deal for the players to get their meals. We still had to pay, on a reduced basis, and you had a ticket that every time you came in to eat they punched so much money off your ticket. At the park we might have a hot dog and a Coke for lunch. We were able to use that meal ticket for dinner, because that was about all the money we had.

Joe could throw hard, but he was wild. He pitched one game while he was with Hamilton, Ontario, and the manager had told him he was staying in to pitch the entire game no matter what happened, that he was going to finish the game. The headlines in the local newspaper the next morning said something to the effect of "Hamilton loses as Linneman walks 14 and strikes out 16."

Albany was a fun team to play for—in the Georgia-Florida League —because we got to travel to some neat places. Tallahassee was in the league, and there was an amusement park there that all of the players really enjoyed. We were young and daring and we didn't know any better. They had big diving boards, and we used to go off of them all the time. We also figured out a way to climb even higher, maybe 50 or 60 feet off the ground, and dive into the water. We'd do it a couple of times, and then somebody would spot us and start yelling and run us out of the area, but we always found a way to get back in.

Because of the war, all of baseball was cutting back on the number of its minor-league teams, and to try to curtail expenses, the Cardinals had all of their minor leaguers report to Lynchburg, Virginia, for spring training in March of 1943.

Spring training was different in those days. It wasn't like today where you have fancy complexes with four or five fields and everybody does their work in a couple of hours and then heads for the golf course. We were all working on one field—maybe 150 guys— and we were out there all day, with only a short break to have some soup for lunch.

Ollie Vanek was running the minor league camp then, and it seemed his idea for everybody to get into shape was to run. We had a one-mile track, and he made everybody go around and around. You would come up to him, and he would just be standing there waving you on saying, "keep going, keep going." You had to keep running until you dropped. I've never seen such a locker room full of sweat-soaked, exhausted guys in my life.

We had very little batting practice, kind of like that tryout camp I had with the Cardinals. We played a lot of pepper, and I guess the guys in charge thought was enough practice to get our batting eyes in shape.

You also had to do a lot more jobs in those days, and you couldn't ever question anyone in authority or even think about not doing what they said or asked you to do. Joe Mathes, the scout who had signed me, and Walter Shannon, another long-time Cardinals executive, were there that spring and they were trying to weed through all of those players. They asked me to help string up a netting around the batting cage and said, "We'll reimburse you for it."

Me and a couple of other guys were out there for about three or four hours getting it set up, and I think they gave each of us a quarter.

When it came time to break camp and assign everybody to teams, I was left in Lynchburg, which was Class B ball. I was playing mostly shortstop, but Mathes and Shannon had told me that spring they thought it would be in my best interests if I learned to play some other positions and moved around a little bit. I was playing some games at second and even some at third, but still mostly was the shortstop.

When we weren't playing or I had some extra time to kill, I walked down to the courthouse and sat in the courtrooms to listen to the cases. It was my version of people watching, and it beat sitting around the lobby of a hotel.

They were mostly small cases, nothing really serious, but it was interesting to watch the reactions of all the people involved.

As it turned out, I only stayed in Lynchburg a couple of weeks. I got off to a great start and was hitting the hell out of the ball. The team in Rochester, one of the Triple A affiliates, was not doing well and then their starting shortstop got hurt. They needed to find a shortstop, and the guys in charge of the minor leagues decided I was the most logical choice to go.

It was a Sunday morning when I got the word I was being sent to Rochester, where one of the old Gas House Gang members, Pepper Martin, was the manager. He had been one of my favorite players growing up, and all I could think of on the train ride to Rochester was what an honor and thrill it was going to be to play for him.

The train trip from Lynchburg to Rochester took all night, and I didn't get much sleep sitting in that seat. The train pulled into Rochester at about 11:30 a.m., and I went straight to the ballpark, old Red Wing Stadium. I went to the office, explained who I was and why I was there, and they told me how to get to the clubhouse.

Remember, I was just 20 years old, and had yet to play a full season in the minor leagues. I was about to join a team with a lot of veteran guys, and I was feeling a little uncertain and out of place as I knocked on the clubhouse door.

The trainer answered, and said, "Who are you?" I was a skinny little kid, looked kind of frail and probably was not what they were expecting in the way of a replacement player. I told him my name was Schoendienst, and he just looked at me kind of funny.

He walked away and went up to Pepper, who was in the middle of a team meeting. "Hey, you got you a little ballplayer here," he yelled to Pepper. Martin walked over, and I could tell he was eyeballing me up and down.

I could hear him muttering and starting to curse. "I've got enough bat boys," he said, turning to renew his attack on his struggling team. I guess he hadn't heard the trainer say who I was, or maybe the trainer didn't offer him my name. I yelled back to Martin, "I'm not a bat boy. I'm a shortstop."

Pepper again stopped the meeting and walked back to where I was standing next to the door.

"You're not that Shone-er something or other that they're sending me?" he said. I answered that I was, and that seemed to upset Martin even more.

"I'm in last place, on a 10-game losing streak, and now they're sending me bat boys, babies," Martin roared.

I probably had expected a little better reception, but Martin probably expected a little older and bigger player as well. I went in and sat down and listened to the rest of the meeting, then Martin came up and sat down next to me.

"So you're my new shortstop," he said. "Well, you're playing."

If I had been nervous before my first game with Union City, that was nothing compared to the butterflies I was experiencing before this game. I was determined not to let it get to me, and just do what I could to try to help the team win, and luckily didn't have a repeat of my first-game troubles a year earlier.

That league also gave me my first lesson in learning to ignore the taunts of fans. We were playing Syracuse, which was a pretty good rival, and some people behind the dugout started to get on me when I was coming up to bat.

"Where did this bum come from?" they yelled. They were on me pretty good and I hadn't even swung the bat yet. I really thought it was going to be rough.

After he got over his initial shock, Pepper seemed pleased to have me around. We developed a pretty good relationship, and it was fun sometimes to watch him get upset and lose his temper, and man did he have a temper.

Some of the people told a story that when he was in the lower minors, he jumped an umpire one time and observers thought he was going to kill him before some other guys were able to pull him away.

Pepper was always playing games. If it was raining and you couldn't take batting practice, he would form teams for a game of touch football. He had a bowling team. If we were on the road and got rained out, he'd get a group of guys together and go bowling. He was always pulling practical jokes on people. I think he was like a big overgrown kid who was just out there having fun. That was the way he had been as a player and he never changed.

I hadn't been in Rochester too long when Pepper came up to me while I was putting on my uniform before a game. He wanted to know if I was wearing a protective cup. I said no, that I had never been able to get used to one. They made me feel uncomfortable. He yelled to one of the workers. "Barney get this kid a cup."

I said, "I can't handle it." Pepper said. "Put it on. If you're going to play the infield you're going to need it or you are going to get hurt." So I put it on.

The game was in Newark, and we were playing the Yankees farm team. They had a guy named Levy, a big, strong kid who could hit the ball hard. I was playing just to the left of second, and he hit a hard smash that hit right off the edge of the grass and it hit me right in the cup and split the cup in half. That was the first day I ever wore a cup, and it was a lifesaver.

Pepper said, "I saved you right there." I said, "You sure did. What else do you want me to do?"

He had a garden behind the left field fence that he kept along with one of the groundskeepers. One day, Pepper got into an argument and got kicked out of the game. He went into the clubhouse, showered, changed into his street clothes and walked back onto the field. He called time, then strolled out toward left field, hopped the fence and into the garden. He got the hose out and just stood there and started watering. There wasn't a darn thing the umpire could do about it except stand there smiling and trying not to laugh too hard.

Another day, we were playing on a Sunday afternoon and had the bases loaded with nobody out in the bottom of the ninth. It was a tie game, and our batter hit a long drive to centerfield. The outfielder caught the ball, but the runner on third came home to score and we all jogged off to the clubhouse, thinking we had won the game.

It was about 10 minutes later when we were all in various degrees of undress, getting ready to shower—including Pepper— when someone came into the clubhouse and told us we had to go back on the field. He said the umpires had ruled our runners on first and second had left the base too early and had been declared out, creating a triple play and wiping out our winning run.

Pepper was about half dressed, but he stormed out of his chair and back onto the field. What was more impressive was he never stopped to open the wooden doors in the tunnel that separated the clubhouse from the dugout. He burst right through them, sending splinters everywhere as he didn't even slow down. That was about as mad as I had ever seen him.

Because this was in an era before expansion, there were a lot of great cities in the International League then. We went to Baltimore, and Toronto and Montreal. One time in Baltimore, I was killing time before going to the ballpark and wandered into a sporting goods store. We had to buy our own bats at the time, and nobody had more than a couple. We weren't making any money, and I was just glad to have a bat and didn't think a whole lot about it.

I picked up some of the bats in the store and began to swing one of them. "This is a pretty good bat," I said. It was brown, and weighed about 32 ounces. It cost 98 cents, and I bought it. I took it to the ballpark and started using it in games and started to hit great. Pepper was playing once in a while, and one day when he was in the lineup he picked up that bat and started to walk up to home plate.

"Pepper, that's my good bat," I yelled to him, "That's OK," he said. "It's got a lot of hits in it." "Well don't break it," I shouted back.

I had had the bat a month. He took one swing and broke it. He said he would buy me a new one, but I told him he wouldn't be able to find out like that. He didn't either, and he never bought me a bat. I had to go back to using my old one.

Walter Alston, who went on to manage the Dodgers all those years, was on that team, as was Steve Mizerak, the pool shark. He would go into the pool halls wherever we were playing, smoking a big cigar, and look like he was just some lost, poor soul. He'd hang around and watch for a while, and pretty soon someone would ask him to get in a game They would wager a quarter or a half dollar or something, then he would run the table and take their money. I really thought someday he was going to get nailed when people caught on to what he was doing, but luckily for him that never happened. I played against Ralph Kiner that year—he was with Toronto—and the competition in that league was the best I had ever faced, and it was a really enjoyable year.

An umpire in the league gave me the nickname "Snowshoes" because the shoes I was wearing during the games were a few sizes too big for me and my feet slapped around in them like snowshoes. Equipment was a lot different than it is now, and one of the biggest differences was the players had to buy everything for themselves.

Most guys only had one glove, and you protected that thing like it was made out of gold. I didn't have money for a new one, so if the laces broke or one of the fingers came undone I would stitch it back up and fix it myself. Later, after I made it to St. Louis, I actually designed a glove myself and gave the pattern to Rawlings, the sporting goods company.

It was a small glove, but it was flat and open. I drew it up on a piece of paper and they made it. The Rawlings people liked it, and said if I would sign a contract they would give me a couple of gloves. I didn't want to get involved with that, so I just paid for the glove and didn't think anything more about it.

The Rawlings people, however, liked the glove so much they put it in the mold and made it themselves and sold a ton of them and made a lot of money on it. I just liked the way the glove felt. That was the only thing I was worried about.

It turned out that I led the International League in hitting that year with a .337 average, not too shabby for a 20-year-old, 155-pound shortstop. I became the youngest person to lead the league in hitting since Wee Willie Keeler in 1892. Considering Pepper Martin had thought I looked like the bat boy when I first showed up at the clubhouse door, I felt I had a pretty good season.

World War II was getting pretty intense, and I didn't think it would be much longer before my name was called by the draft board. Part of the reason I had not been ordered into the service earlier was my bad eye, which really disqualified me for a lot of the service requirements, as did the fact that four of my brothers were already in the Army.

It's unusual for five brothers in one family to all be in the service at one time, but we were. My four brothers were all overseas as well, and luckily they all came home safely. None of them, in fact, were even wounded. We were really fortunate.

Andy was a medic, working in Greenland. Eugene was in Japan, Julius was in Germany working with the commandos, and Elmer also was in Germany, working in a tank division. They all had some really dangerous and scary experiences, and none of them really like to talk much about the war.

The Cardinals were convinced, correctly as it turned out, that I was going to enter the Army sometime in 1944 so they didn't want to mess with me trying to come up to the majors, but wanted to wait until my service commitment was over. After I spent another winter working for the highway department in Illinois, they sent me back to Rochester to begin the 1944 season.

Because of the success I had enjoyed the year before, the people in Rochester were happy to see me back. They knew I was headed for the Army soon, and my papers did come and I was ordered to report to Camp Blanding, Florida, where they were training infantry soldiers as replacements for the troops fighting in Europe.

Before I left Rochester, the fans passed the hat the night of my final game, taking up a collection in appreciation for what I had done for the ballclub. The fans collected $425, which was really a nice gesture on their part and something I really appreciated. I was glad they enjoyed the way I played. In the 25 games I played that spring, I hit .373.

We were playing Montreal, and everybody on both teams knew I was leaving the next day. We were losing by a score of 12-1 or 10-1 or something like that, and when I came up to bat for the last time, the catcher said to me, "How would you like a nice fat one, right down the alley?"

I didn't know if he was kidding or not, but I said that would be great. The next pitch came in straight right down the middle. I took a helluva cut, and popped straight up, right to the catcher.

Joining the Army was not something I was real excited about, but I knew I didn't have any choice. Training for the infantry, we were exposed to just about every situation you can imagine—how to wire for mines, how to blow up bridges, how to set booby traps and dig up mines. They used powder instead of gunpowder in the practice mines, so if you tried to disarm it and it blew up, you wouldn't get killed. It pinched your hand pretty good, but that was all. Some of the guys figured out how to dislodge the wire so it wouldn't hurt them. The lieutenant tried to tell them the only ones they were hurting by doing that was themselves. If they were sent to Europe into the front lines and had to disarm a mine and didn't know how to do it, they were going to get killed and so were a lot of their buddies.

When we weren't learning combat stuff, we were learning how to survive in the swamps in Florida, surrounded by deadly snakes and alligators. Playing baseball seemed a long way away during those days.

The war was far enough along that luckily most of the people I was in training with never went overseas, including myself. We were transferred from Camp Blanding to Pine Camp, New York, right outside of Watertown, where all of the Italian prisoners of war were being held captive.

The situation there was much better, because one of our jobs was to build ballfields so we could keep the prisoners entertained and give them something to do. We also put together a camp team, looking over all of the charts to see which of the soldiers had played before. We played on weekends, traveling to some of the other nearby Army bases. One weekend we went to New York to play some games on Governor's Island, and had to stay over in the city.

Our lieutenant told us we would be staying at the Roosevelt Hotel, but when we got there, they didn't have our reservations. We called the lieutenant, and he said, "Oh, I knew it was some president's name. You're staying at the Lincoln Hotel."

The only bad part about my stay in the Army was I hurt my right shoulder during one of our ballgames. I was stealing second, made a headfirst slide, and jammed the shoulder into a shin. The injury was later diagnosed as a shallow shoulder socket, and it occasionally would pop out of place. Even when it was in place, it affected my throwing and made me develop a motion where I just kind of whipped the ball, with a sidearm or almost underhand delivery. Playing in Rochester a year earlier, I had been chasing a pop foul and had slammed the shoulder into the grandstand wall. That was the start of my shoulder problems.

A few years later, I slipped in a game one day and landed on my shoulder, throwing it out of place. One time I even threw it out of joint by just making a move to try to tag a baserunner. It seemed like it was sore almost all the time.

The shoulder might have gotten better while I was still in the Army, except one of our training exercises was firing bazooka guns, and the recoil of that gun went straight into my shoulder, never giving it a complete chance to heal.

I was working in the supply office during the Cardinals-Browns World Series in 1944, and got to hear most of it on the radio. I didn't know the players, since the major league and minor league spring training camps were in different sites in those days, but I still wanted the Cardinals to win.

I didn't know at the time how close I was to getting out of the Army, and that I would be with the Cardinals just a few months later. Doctors decided my eye injury and my shoulder were enough of a combination that I was able to get a medical discharge.

The discharge came through in time for me to go home for a little while and rest before leaving to join the Cardinals in spring training, 1945. My dream of becoming a major leaguer was about to come true.

Chapter 4

A MAJOR LEAGUER

Because of the war, all major league teams had moved their spring training camps closer to their regular-season homes. Instead of going to Florida, the Cardinals' camp was in Cairo, Illinois.

We found out why spring training is usually in Florida or Arizona—it rained so much that spring that the Mississippi and Ohio Rivers flooded and we got flooded out. We were staying in the old Cairo Hotel and it rained so much we couldn't even get out to the field. It could have been worse—if it hadn't been for the dams, the water could have reached the third floor windows of the hotel.

It didn't take many days of being forced to just sit around the hotel before the men in charge decided this wasn't working, and loaded all of us and the equipment back up and headed for St. Louis, where we completed spring training at Sportsman's Park.

The Browns had some of the same problems. They were training in Cape Girardeau and we played them a few times but mostly just played intrasquad games among ourselves. Spring training always has been one of the best times of the year during a baseball season, but that year was an exception.

Back then, spring training was a lot different than it is today. When you were a minor leaguer, just a kid starting out, the coaches and instructors talked to you for what seemed like hours on end. You couldn't wait to get out of that little room, sitting on those hard stools, and get out on the field and start playing ball. It was always so cramped and humid in that room with all of those guys there. Spring training was a lot more disciplined then. They told you what you were going to do, how you were going to do it, then made certain that's what you went out and did. Nobody questioned authority back then; if somebody in charge told you to do something, you did it, no questions asked.

Of course that's the way society was as well, and all of the problems that have come along in baseball the last 25 years or so are a reflection of the problems that have come along in society in that same time span. It's a lot tougher to be a parent now than it was then, I think, and it's a lot tougher to be a coach or a manager as well. You almost have to be a psychologist and counselor in addition to knowing when to put on the hit and run or the suicide squeeze.

We spent a lot of time working on fundamentals. We worked in groups, practicing cutoff plays and rundowns and other situations. We didn't spend nearly as much time hitting as players do today. We played a lot of pepper, spent a lot of time on fielding drills and sliding. It seemed as if you did everything for hours at a time.

Part of the difference was that we only had one field, where today the new complexes have four or five fields, plus batting cages and extra pitching mounds. We would be ready to go by 9 a.m., then get out on the field after the morning talk from the manager and coaches, and we wouldn't be done for the day until 4 p.m., taking only a half-hour or so off for lunch. If you wanted to today, you could get the same amount of work in and get practice over for the day in an hour or two.

We didn't just stand around and watch other guys on the field, however. We were always doing something—playing catch, playing pepper, keeping busy.

When it comes to learning and being able to execute fundamentally sound baseball, the players in my day probably had an edge over the players of today for one simple reason—experience. We probably worked on fundamentals a little more than the players do today, but the biggest difference is guys get to the major leagues so much quicker today they haven't had the time in the minor leagues necessary to develop those instinctive skills of knowing what to do with the ball when it is hit to them, and the knowledge of how to properly execute every kind of play in every possible situation. Players who haven't spent a lot of time in the minor leagues can't know those things because there is only one way you learn it, and that's from experience.

We talked about the game more back then than players do today. Everybody always knew the score, the inning, how many outs there were, where the runners were, who was batting. They don't seem to do that as much today.

Most players spent a lot of time in the minors. I was an exception, coming up to the majors in just about a year and a half, which was really quick then or today. Part of the reason I think I was able to move up so quickly and succeed at an early age was because of my knowledge of fundamentals, relying on skills I think I was just born with and the knowledge I received at a very early age playing for Ed Roach in Germantown. Everything he taught me came into use later on.

The one thing I've never figured out about batting practice anyway is what the big deal is about it. The pitch is coming in at only about 60 miles an hour, and I don't see how that's going to prepare you to hit a guy throwing 85 mph or a wicked curveball when the game begins. We were better off spending all of our practice time working to develop other skills.

It was an exciting time to join the Cardinals, only months after they had won the World Series. The team still was missing a lot of regulars who had gone into the service, and I knew that was going to help my chances of making the club.

One thing I wasn't certain of was where I would be playing. I had mostly been a shortstop in the minors, even though Wally Shannon and Joe Mathes had stressed to me the importance of playing second base and other positions. I preferred shortstop, but that was one spot that wasn't available in the spring of 1945, not as long as Marty Marion was wearing a Cardinals' uniform.

Marty was a great player, one of the best to ever wear a Cardinals' uniform, and he was so smooth on defense that he was a real pleasure to watch. I learned a lot of things watching him, and when I got a chance to play alongside him at either second base or third, it made my job much easier knowing he was standing next to me and would almost certainly get to any ball that was out of my range.

A lot of rookies in my situation might have been in awe because there were so many great players on the Cardinals, even though guys like Stan Musial, Terry Moore and Enos Slaughter were not there, having gone into the service. For some reason, meeting famous players like that never was hard for me. I appreciated their ability and was honored to meet them, to play with them and to get to know them, but I was never impressed by them. Not too many things get me excited, including meeting famous players.

My biggest problem that spring was figuring out where I should play. I had never sat on the bench in my life, and I didn't want to sit now just to say I was in the major leagues. With Marion at shortstop, I had to look at other options, and one spot I knew manager Billy Southworth was undecided about was left field.

I was working mostly in the infield, but one day after practice I asked coach Mike Gonzalez, who was from Cuba, if he would hit me some fungos in the outfield. I probably hadn't played there since I was a kid, but I didn't think it would be that difficult of an adjustment.

One concern I had about playing the outfield was how well I would be able to throw from there since my arm was still sore from when I injured it in the Army. I just decided I would give it my best shot and see what happened.

Everything Gonzalez hit in the air, I was able to track down and catch. He didn't even notice I was just lobbing the ball back in to him.

After he had hit balls to me for quite a while, Gonzalez noticed Southworth walking by on his way off the field and yelled out to him, all excited, talking in his broken English like he always did.

"Beel," he said to Southworth. "We no need to worry about left field anymore. This Red, he great, play left field, catch everything. You watch what Mike tell you."

Gonzalez resumed hitting fungos, and I still made all of the plays with Southworth watching. From that moment on, I was a left fielder—unless there was an injury on the infield or Marion needed to take a day off to rest.

We opened the season in Chicago, against the Cubs, and I found myself in the starting lineup, playing left field, batting third. With one out, Johnny Hopp singled and stole second, bringing me up to bat for the first time in the major leagues. Paul Derringer was on the mound for Chicago, a tough righthander with a high leg kick. It would make a nice story to say I homered or at least got a hit to drive in the run, but unfortunately I grounded out to first, although Hopp did advance to third. He was stranded there as Walker Cooper also grounded to first.

The nerves bouncing around inside my body were nothing different than any other kid making his major-league debut It's always interesting to watch guys come up in that situation, because you remember what it was like for you as well.

The only thing a kid in that situation worries about is trying not to mess up. You don't want to make any mistakes, you don't want to miss any signs, and consequently that makes you tense up, and the first thing you do is screw up. The hardest skill for a young player to master in the major leagues is to relax and learn that he is playing the same game he has been playing ever since he was a kid, and that's the way he has to approach it. He can't all of a sudden do something different or change the way he has been playing all his life simply because he has reached the major leagues.

What made my first game a little harder than normal is that I was in an unfamiliar position, left field. I had to wait until the Cubs' second batter was up to get my first fielding chance, a routine fly ball that I caught easily.

I wasn't as fortunate in the fourth inning. Phil Cavarreta, a tough hitter, lined a shot toward me. Reports in the newspaper the next day said I misjudged the ball in the brisk wind, and I guess that's probably as good an explanation as any. I really just flat-out missed it, the ball bouncing off my hands, and it was ruled a two-base error. The error led to the second Chicago run of the game.

As I said, once you screw up and make a mistake, that puts even more pressure on you. That was the emotional battle I had to fight for the rest of the game, thinking more than once about the advice Branch Rickey had given me after my bad start in my opening game in the minors. If I could get a hit, it would take some of that load off my shoulders.

I was 0-for-3 when I came up to bat in the eighth, probably for the final time in the game. This time, I got a pitch I liked and slammed it for a triple, my first hit. I trotted home a few moments later on a single by Walker Cooper to tie the game at 2.

Unfortunately, we lost the game, 3-2, when the Cubs scored a run in the bottom of the ninth.

The easiest way for a young player—or even a veteran—to relax is to get off to a good start. If you're a young player, a quick start will provide the confidence that you can play and have success at the major-league level. Even for veterans, it's nice to know your skills are still sharp, and the season is off to a positive start. Every season, getting that first base hit is a major confidence booster. It always made me mad when I didn't get at least one hit on opening day. I needed that first hit to relax me and make me ready for the season to begin.

It was even worse as a rookie, because you know more people are looking at you, watching you, wondering how you are going to do. The older players want to make certain you are a good guy and a good player, and the management wants to make certain you are ready for the majors and don't need more time to season in the minors. That's a lot of pressure to put on a young kid, and some are able to succeed and some aren't.

The older guys also want to find out just how hard they can push a rookie, to see how much he will take. It wasn't unusual back then for a rookie to have to get out of the way of a 90-mile-an-hour fastball that came in just under his chin. The way he reacts to a wakeup call like that was important in shaping opinions of what other players thought of the kid.

There was a lot more bench jockeying going on in those days then there is today, and it was especially aimed at rookies. Some of the insults were harmless, like calling a rookie a bum, but it was all done with the intention of finding out how far a guy could be pushed before he reacted and exploded.

In addition to having problems throwing the ball because of my sore arm, I was having trouble with my eye again, trying to see the ball when I was hitting. Joe Linneman came by to visit one day, and I confessed to him I thought the problems were getting worse. He convinced me I needed to mention it to the Cardinals and see if they could get me some help.

Joe Mathes and Wally Shannon, my two advisers and confidants, had a friend in south St. Louis who was an eye doctor, Dr. Mueller, and they sent me to see him. He ran all of the tests, and found out my vision out of my left eye was indeed still affected by my old injury. There was a spot in my eye, and I was always shaking my head trying to see if I could clear it.

Dr. Mueller prescribed some eye exercises for me to do, and I spent a long time every day doing what he had instructed me to do. The vision in the eye finally improved to 20/35, a big help when I was trying to bat. Sometimes I wish I had been able to hit in the major leagues with perfect vision in both eyes. I'm sure I would have been better.

I didn't develop any close friendships on the team during that year, probably because I just kept to myself and kept my mouth shut. I got along with everybody, but never went out of my way to make certain I was with somebody at all times. Everybody pulled together on that team and rooted for one another, and I never remember anybody on that team criticizing another player. It was just something that wasn't done.

Even though I had been living away from home for a couple of years and playing baseball, the major leagues was a totally different world, just as it is today. We traveled by train, and went to all of the exciting towns like New York, Philadelphia, Boston and Chicago. It was just as I had dreamed it would be, and the whole year I think I was pinching myself to believe it was really happening to me.

You always get a little touch of reality from time to time. On one of my first trips to Chicago, I went to church late and arrived at Wrigley Field alone after the rest of the team was there. When I got to the gate where the players entered the park, the attendant just looked at me and glared.

"Go 'way kid," he told me. "Don't be givin' me that line. I've heard everything."

There wasn't any way I was going to convince him that I really did play for the Cardinals, so I turned away and found the door to the Cubs' offices. There, the attendant was much more accommodating, looking at my identification card and then directing me down some back stairs to the Cardinals' locker room.

Three weeks later, we were in Brooklyn, and I had a similar run-in with another overbearing gate attendant.

"Go on, you bum, don't be trying any funny business around here," he told me. That time, one of the other players on our team came along at just the right time and convinced the attendant that I was indeed a player on the Cardinals. Looking at it objectively, I can see where they thought I was trying to pull a fast one. I did look younger than my age, just a skinny, freckle-faced kid, and there wasn't as much recognition of players from other teams in different cities as there is today because we weren't on television all the time.

When we were at home, I lived with Joe Linneman's parents, who had moved to St. Louis by then, to a house near Tower Grove Park. Joe was still in the service. That was a big break for me. I only had to walk two or three blocks, where I caught the streetcar that ran up and down Grand Ave. It took me right to the ballpark, and I was able to come home the same way. I didn't have to pay rent and didn't have to worry about transportation, and that saved a rookie making probably $3,000 or $4,000 for the entire season a lot of money.

Going home on the streetcar one day after a game near the end of the season, in September, two ladies came up to me and one of them said, "Red, you played a wonderful game." I thanked her, and when the streetcar reached my stop, I got off and walked back to the Linneman's house.

I had told my friend, Mary Wolf, about a dream I had about meeting a red-headed baseball player. When we went to the game, we saw Marty Marion, who had auburn hair, and I told Mary, "That's not him." On the streetcar, we saw Red, and I said, "That's him." After we met him, we stayed on the streetcar to see where he got off, and found out he lived right in the same neighborhood. When I got home, I went in and woke my father up and said, "Who do you think I met tonight?" When I told him, he approved of him then.

—Mary Schoendienst

Mary was in a restaurant, Pelican's, in the neighborhood the next night when I happened to walk in. I saw her, and walked over to her table and said, "I forgot to get your name." She told me, and gave me her phone number, and I said I would call her in a couple of days. Only a few days later, I bumped into her again, this time at Mass on Sunday at St. Margaret's Church.

Linneman, who had returned from the service and was working as a mechanic at a service station at the corner of 22nd and Olive, had been dating a girl, Babe, whom he later married. Joe thought it would be fun if we went on a double date.

I was on a month's leave, and after Babe and I had gone out, I said to Red, "Why don't you get a date and we'll all go out." He said he didn't know whom he could get, but then he said, "I met a gal on the streetcar who lives down on Lafayette. I'll call her." It was Mary, and she said she would go.

My brother and I had an old 1935 Chevrolet and we went and picked Mary up and drove over to the Olde English Inn in East St. Louis, down near the stockyards. We had a great time, and decided to go out again. Just as we picked up Mary, the car broke down. Mary said we could take her car, and it turned out it was a 1941 Red

Ford convertible. We thought we were hot stuff in that car. We walked off and left my old Chevy sitting on Grand Avenue.

— Joe Linneman

Meeting Mary really was a nice way to top off my rookie season. It had been a good year, as I hit .278, drove in 47 runs and actually led the league with 26 stolen bases. We finished second, three games behind the Cubs, but still won 95 games. I knew it was against some weaker competition, since a lot of the good players had been serving in the military, and I was looking forward to seeing how I would fare against them when they returned in 1946.

Even the stars weren't making much money in those days, so almost every player had to find another job in the winter to tide him over until spring training began again. I had to work almost every winter, and I had a variety of jobs. I wasn't married and didn't have a family to support, so I moved back to Germantown and went back to work for the state highway department, operating a jackhammer. Having a job like that really made you appreciate the fact you played baseball for the principle part of your living.

That also was a time when you couldn't be too picky over whatever job you had. There was a lot of competition for every job available, and you were lucky if you got one, since employers knew you would be quitting in only a few months. After I started staying in St. Louis over the winter, I had jobs working in a department store selling shirts or shoes. Later I went to work for an independent packing company, doing a lot of promotional work. That was a more enjoyable job.

Spending a lot of time with Mary that winter also was enjoyable. She was a great fan, and that helped our relationship. Her father, Jimmie, was a postal clerk and a big sports fan. He even kept young Mary out of school for a day in 1934, deciding a trip to watch the World Champion Cardinals being honored in a parade was a good education for his young daughter. That sealed her future as a baseball fan.

Red had a favorite spot, Brownies, on the corner of Arsenal and Grand. We'd get our exercise by running all the way across Tower Grove Park, then we'd sit at the bar until 10:30 or 11. Then it was time to go, and we'd run all the way back across the park. We'd get our exercise for the day, and sit at the bar for three hours.

— Joe Linneman

That winter, Southworth got an offer to jump to Boston to become manager of the Braves and he took it. The Cardinals chose Eddie Dyer to become the new manager, and as I boarded the train headed for spring training in St. Petersburg, I wondered what the change in managers would mean for me.

More importantly, the biggest change would be in the squad assembling for spring training. The war was over, and all of the stars were back, including Musial, Moore and Slaughter. Musial would likely be going back to his spot in left field, where I had played the most in 1945, and the one thing I knew was that I didn't want to be sent back to the minors or have to spend most of the time sitting on the bench, waiting for a chance to play.

Dyer, whom I had known first in the minor leagues, came over to talk to me the day I reported to St. Petersburg.

"Kid," he called me. "You're going to pinch-hit and pinch-run this year. You're going to be my number one reserve."

That wasn't exactly the news I was hoping to hear, and the only thing it did was convince me that I was going to play harder than ever to work my way into a starting position.

Whitey Kurowski had been our regular third baseman the year before, and he was involved in a contract dispute with Mr. Breadon so he didn't show up in camp on time. Dyer put me at third, and I played pretty well. Still, when Whitey finally showed up, he reclaimed the position.

Marion was experiencing some aches and pains then, so Dyer moved me over to shortstop. When Marion was able to return in a couple of weeks, I had played well enough to convince Dyer that I belonged in the lineup and that my best position probably was going to be second base.

I was rooming with Max Lanier, and I knew something was going on because he kept acting a little jumpy. The Pasquel boys had come up from Mexico and were talking with all of the stars about jumping to a new league they were going to start down there. They had suitcases stuffed full of money they were showing off, and some of the players, like Lanier, were thinking hard about taking the money and running.

They talked to Musial, but he turned them down. Three guys off our team—Lanier, Lou Klein and pitcher Freddie Martin—agreed to take the money and left the Cardinals.

Klein was upset because he had been the regular second baseman and I had kind of taken his job. Lanier and Martin just looked at as a chance to make some more money, but unfortunately for them, the deal went bad from the start and never worked out.

Lanier never actually told me he was leaving, but left me a note in our hotel room one night. "I'm leaving and keep hitting line drives. Hope to play against you."

With Klein gone, my main competition to play was out of the way and it relaxed me a little more and let me concentrate on just doing my job and helping the club win. I was lucky enough to make the All-Star team for the first time, and going into that NL clubhouse for the game in Boston was a real treat, sitting among the greatest players in the game. The teams were picked by the managers and writers, so it was almost more of an honor to be selected then than it is today, when the fans vote. Fans don't always go by the stats, and who is having the best year, but the managers and writers tend to notice that a little more and pick players they think are deserving of the honor.

There are some players now who get picked for the game and turn it down, saying they would rather have the three days off. I can't imagine any of the players of my era doing that. If you were picked to go, you went. The President usually came to the game, and it seemed as if it was a bigger honor back then.

Our race against the Dodgers came down to the final day of the season, and if we had beaten the Cubs on the last day we would have won the pennant outright. Instead we lost, and that forced us into a playoff—at the time a best two-out-of-three series.

A coin flip was used to determine the site of the opener, and Dodgers' manager Leo Durocher won the toss and chose to host the final two games, putting the opening game in Sportsman's Park.

Howie Pollet pitched a strong game, and we won, 4-2. We were a confidant bunch on the train ride to New York, and the one thing we were certain of was that we wanted to finish the series off the next game. We didn't want Brooklyn getting the momentum back by winning and forcing the third and deciding game.

We jumped on the Dodgers quickly, building an 8-1 lead before they rallied to make it 8-4. They loaded the bases with one out, and the fans were going crazy. But Harry Brecheen came out of the bullpen to strike out the last two batters and put us into the World Series.

Almost all season, I had been trying to make arrangements to buy my first car. Mary was working as a receptionist at a Ford dealership, and she said she could help me get a car. Cars were hard to come by at the time, not like they are today. The folks at the dealer kept putting me off, and I was getting tired of it.

I had another friend, Mr. Brumley, who was a good fan. He worked at Wilcox Buick, on Vandeventer, and he kept saying he could fix me up with a car. His seats were right next to the on-deck circle at Sportsman's Park, and he would always talk with the players while they were waiting to hit.

Mr. Brumley kept trying to talk me into it, but I kept telling him a Buick was too big for me. I was still single, and I didn't need that big a car. Finally, after I was getting tired of waiting for the Ford people to come through, I told him OK.

"I can't get a car anywhere," I told him. He said, "This is your last chance. I have a car, and I'll save it for you." This was right before we left for the playoff game in Brooklyn, and he told me he would have it waiting for me when we got back. I called him that morning from Brooklyn, and said we would be coming in late, but he said he would be waiting for me.

We won, and got on the train, and the whole ride back to St. Louis I think I was thinking about two things, going to the World Series and getting that car. When the train pulled into Union Station, everybody else grabbed their bags and headed through the doors into the lobby, where a big mob of people was waiting. I pulled my suitcase off the train, hopped the tracks to the street, jumped in a cab and headed for Wilcox Buick.

Mr. Brumley was waiting for me and he said, "They're just getting it shined up for you." It was a Roadmaster, a great car. I handed him a check for $2,100—the total price. I never bought anything unless I could pay for it. If I can't pay for it I don't want it. I'm still that way. I don't like to borrow anything.

He had the license and everything all set up for me, and I jumped in the car and drove to Germantown to see my mom and show off the car. I took her for a ride, saw some of my friends, then headed back to the city. I kept that car for a couple of years. It only had 27,000 miles on it when I sold it. I kept in contact with Mr. Brumley for a few years, until he moved to California.

It took a while for both events to sink in—that I finally owned a car, and that I was going to the World Series. It was just my second year in the majors, and some players go their entire careers without playing in the Series. It didn't seem that far removed from the time Joe and I were racing to the ice cream parlor after school to check the scores of the games. Now all the folks in Germantown, including my mom and dad, were going to be huddled around their radios listening to me and the rest of the Cardinals.

For some reason, I wasn't nervous when the Series began. I guess it was because I felt all the pressure was off. Our goal when the season began was to win the National League pennant and get to the World Series, and we had done that. Nobody really thought about winning the Series, but I also thought as long as were there, we should win it.

All of the reporters were making the Series out to be a personal battle between Musial and Ted Williams, two of the greatest players the game has known. Even though baseball is very much an individualistic game, it's tough for an entire team to rise or fall on one player's performance, and that was the case in this matchup.

Eddie Dyer decided our best hope of trying to contain Williams was to use an unorthodox shift that had three infielders to the right side of second base, leaving only the third baseman to guard the entire area between second and third. He knew Williams' tendencies to hit the ball to the right side, and was betting on the fact that Ted also was vain enough that he would not try to beat the shift by simply poking the ball through the openings on the left side of the field.

The gamble paid off. Williams got five hits in the series, all singles, and was one of the most frustrated people I've ever seen as the Series came down to a dramatic finish. The Series was made famous by Enos Slaughter's mad dash around the bases in the seventh game, scoring all the way from first on what should have been a single by Harry Walker. It was scored a double because Walker went to second on the throw to the plate, but that was only because of Slaughter's mad dash. We were ahead, 4-3, going to the ninth inning.

The Red Sox mounted a threat, putting two runners on with two outs. The next batter, pinch-hitter Tom McBride, hit a slow roller toward me that looked as if it would be an easy chance. Instead, just as I went to field the ball, it took a crazy hop and I blocked the ball with my left shoulder. Luckily I was able to trap it, and flipped the ball to Marion covering second for the final out. As we started to celebrate the World Series championship, people began to refer to that play as the "$40,000 assist" because the $40,000 was the approximate difference between the total shares for the winning team and the losing side. The players' share was about $28,000.

Mary was sitting in the stands, watching the game with her family. We had talked about getting married, but she still hadn't officially been granted her family's blessing. One of the people at the game was her grandfather, Patrick O'Reilly.

> *He was still not sure about Red, until he made that play. After the ball hit him in the chest, then rolled up his arm, and he still made the play and we won the game, then my grandfather said, "You can marry him now." He had not been too happy about that "German" I was going to marry.*
>
> —*Mary Schoendienst*

Some people think that 1946 team was one of the greatest Cardinals' clubs of all time, and it's hard to argue with them. Musial was the leader, of course, but the captain of the team was Terry Moore, the centerfielder. Terry never shouted or raised his voice, but you knew he meant something when he said it. If he didn't think a guy had run fast enough to first base, he would just walk up to him in the dugout and say something like, "You didn't run as fast as you can. Let's put out a little more." He didn't have to shout, he had that kind of control.

It was different back then, however, because players really didn't need somebody yelling at them or trying to motivate them to go all out all the time. They had internal pride and discipline to do it, because they knew if management didn't think they were doing the job, they would not hesitate for a moment to pull a player out of the minor leagues to take their place. If you had a sprained ankle, you had better get it taped up and not tell anybody and not let it affect your play or you might be gone.

There also was a little more pride in the uniform you wore, and viewing baseball not really as a game but as a battle between your side and the opponents. Because players did not change clubs as frequently, there weren't as many relationships built with players from other teams. You never really fraternized with players on the other teams. There really was a feeling that they were the enemy, and they were what stood in the way of you getting where you wanted to be, the World Series.

Branch Rickey was a masterful negotiator in using the goal of reaching the World Series as an incentive to your contract, first when he was with the Cardinals and later when he went to Brooklyn. Every time you came in to talk about your contract before the season began—not very many players had agents in those days—Rickey always would say, "Well, we've got a pretty good ballclub and if you play hard and things work out we've got a pretty good chance of making it to the World Series, which means a nice bonus on your contract." Then when he would tell you how much he was offering you for the season, which really was pretty close to what you were going to get, it almost seemed like he was including the World Series bonus to make it seem like a bigger contract. Even after Rickey went to the Dodgers, Sam Breadon had much the same stance when it came to negotiating contracts.

I don't think Rickey would be as powerful or as successful today as he was during his generation. He knew baseball, and he was a great evaluator of talent, but he also had complete control and that was the way he liked it. When Commissioner Landis ruled the Cardinals had an unfair advantage because of their many farm teams and took some players away from the organization, like Pete Reiser, it really hurt Rickey. He couldn't figure out why somebody else had the right and authority to tell him how to run his business, and why he couldn't do things the way he wanted. He would have some real trouble trying to deal with some of the people running the game today.

Rickey also was lucky with the Cardinals because the team had some great players, led by Musial, who also turned out to be my best friend in the game and one of the closest people to me in the world.

Stan was in the service when I joined the Cardinals in 1945, and we didn't meet until the first day of spring training in 1946. He was from a small town, Donora, Pennsylvania, and we really had a lot of the same values and ideas about baseball and life that we seemed to pick up on and share almost immediately.

It wasn't long before we became roommates, and we stayed there long after we each could have requested a single room on the road. We enjoyed each other's company, and our families later would develop a great relationship that still exists today.

Stan tells the story of how we became roommates, because he was having trouble with the other guy he was rooming with.

After every game he (the roommate) went to the bar. I didn't drink in those days. I didn't like beer. I'd have a beer, and he'd have three or four. I wanted to go eat dinner, and he wanted to sit there and drink. I finally told Leo Ward, our traveling secretary, to get me another roommate. That's how I got Red. The good thing about him was he didn't snore.

—Stan Musial

It really was amazing how much Stan and I had in common. His father had worked in a zinc factory and had taught Stan the value of hard work. Stan also came from a large family, and they were not financially well off, either. He also had overcome a serious injury in the minors that had threatened to end his career just as it was beginning.

Stan and I quickly learned we both liked to take our time unwinding after a game, talking about what had happened and why, and enjoying a nice leisurely dinner in a good restaurant. When we were in New York, we enjoyed going to Broadway shows.

The fastest man I ever saw getting showered and dressed after a game was Enos Slaughter. That shouldn't have surprised me, because he did everything in a hurry. In the time that it took me to unfasten the shoelaces on my spikes, it seemed he had showered, dressed and left the ballpark. I couldn't get in that big of a hurry.

Sitting around the clubhouse for a while, then relaxing and going out to dinner seemed to release the tensions of the game for me, and when I was ready for bed, the game was over and forgotten and I could enjoy a nice night. If I had tried to get out of the clubhouse as quickly as Slaughter, there would not have been any way I could have forgotten about the game that fast.

That's another thing that has changed about the game today, and part of the reason is the abundance of night games instead of day games. It's a lot easier to sit around the clubhouse for a couple of hours when it's 4 o'clock in the afternoon and not 11 o'clock at night. Now, if you walk into a clubhouse 30 minutes after a game ends, almost everyone is gone. Having that time together in the clubhouse really was a major factor in the bonding of a team, and it's a shame today's players don't get to enjoy that feeling.

I was lucky having Stan for a roommate, too, because he was such a good player and so famous that all of the really famous entertainers and celebrities wanted to meet him and be seen with him. Since I usually was with him, that meant I got included as well.

We always used to go to Toots Shor's restaurant in New York, and he always was able to help us get tickets to the good shows we wanted to see, and introduced us to a lot of important people. Later in both of our careers, we were at Chasen's Restaurant in Los Angeles one night when the manager came up to Stan and said there were a couple of people in the restaurant who had recognized him and would like to meet him if it was OK with Stan.

Stan said OK, bring them up, and up to our table walked Jack Benny and George Burns. That would not have happened if Stan had not been so famous.

Some of the people we ran into didn't know who Stan—or I— were, but they still came away with a story to tell.

One night we had gone to Toots Shor's restaurant and a show, and were walking down the street afterward when a panhandler approached us. They were all over the place, and the best thing you could do was ignore them. Stan was already married, so his money was going to his family. I was still single, but I wasn't making any money to speak of anyway, so we almost always tried to avoid the panhandlers whenever we could.

On this night, however, this guy just kept after us saying, "I need money to eat." He was crying these big crocodile tears. Stan is such a sentimental softee anyway, this guy got to him. He reached in his pocket and pulled out a $5 bill and handed it to him. The guy should have been grateful, because that was a lot of money back then. But he kept walking along side of us, telling Stan, "This isn't enough, it's not enough."

Then he started crying again. He made Stan feel so bad that he started crying too, and he gave him another $5. Finally the guy was satisfied and walked away.

After he had a couple of minutes to think about it, Stan looked at me and said, "Why didn't you give him anything, Red?" I had my answer ready. "He didn't ask me for anything," I told Stan.

Being with Stan was just a natural way to meet celebrities. There were nights at Toots Shor's when sitting at the next table would be people like Joe E. Lewis, Jackie Gleason and Don Ameche. All of the celebrities back then were baseball fans, and they all wanted to meet Stan. One of the biggest Cardinal fans around at the time was Harry James, the bandleader. A young Frank Sinatra was singing with his band. James used to wear his Cardinals' jacket on stage, and he would book his band for two weeks in St. Petersburg during March so he could be there for spring training.

Stan is such a personal guy. A lot of times, he and I would go visit kids in hospitals whenever we were on the road in Philadelphia, Pittsburgh or someplace. He didn't want publicity for it and he didn't do it to seek recognition or humanitarian awards, he just did it because he thought it was the right thing to do and he enjoyed making other people happy and maybe giving them a small ray of sunshine to brighten up their lives. That was the kind of guy he was as a player, and he is still that kind of guy today.

One of the celebrities I had an opportunity to meet because of Stan had a different reputation when he played—Ty Cobb. He used to call Stan when we played in New York, and one time the three of us went out to breakfast, and there I was, talking baseball with Ty Cobb. We talked about a lot of different things, and I remember asking his advice on how to get out of a batting slump. He also thought home runs got too much attention, that being able to get hits and drive in runs should be worth just as much notice. I wonder what he would think today about the way the press devotes so much attention to Mark McGwire and Ken Griffey Jr.

About slumps, I was really interested in what Cobb had to say. He said his secret to break out if he was in a rut was to bunt the ball a few times. He said bunting forced you to keep your eye on the ball until it hit the ball, and that's probably the mistake you were making that put you in a slump, not watching the ball all the way until it hit the bat.

Cobb told me, "How many times have you bunted to advance the runner to second or third and thought, 'I really wish he would have let me hit that ball.' That's because you saw the pitch so good. You squared around to bunt, and you watched the ball. That's what you have to do to get out of a slump."

Another great I got a chance to hang out with occasionally was Joe DiMaggio. Because the Yankees and Cardinals both were based in St. Petersburg for spring training, there were many nights we would all be out and would run into each other, usually in a pool hall on Central Ave. DiMaggio was a pretty good pool player along with being one of the greatest baseball players in the history of the game.

In all my years rooming with Stan, there was only one time I saw him get mad and lose his temper. He had one admirer who always called and offered to give us rides to the ballpark. Stan kept turning him down, but the guy didn't get the hint and kept calling.

We had a particularly long game one night, and we didn't get back to the hotel and into bed until after 2 a.m. The guy came around early the next morning, pounding on the door, saying he was there to drive us to the ballpark. Stan had been sleeping soundly, and was mad that the guy had awakened him. He had always tried to be nice and not offend the guy, but this time he yelled out, "Scram fellow, and don't be bothering us anymore." The guy never came back.

Led by Musial, and knowing how well we had played in 1946, the players on the Cardinals thought we would be celebrating a lot more World Series' triumphs in the coming years. As it turned out, of course, the team didn't get back there again until 18 years later, 1964. If you had asked anybody on the team as spring training began in 1947 what they would have been willing to wager on that possibility, you might have become a rich man. We came close, finishing second for three consecutive years, including the 1949 season, when we only lost to Brooklyn by a game.

I didn't know it at the time, but there apparently was some talk between Breadon and Dyer early in the 1947 season about whether the club should trade me. I had not gotten off to a good start, and neither had the club, losing 11 of its first 13 games and falling into last place. Breadon was starting to panic, and looking for explanations about why a world championship team could be playing so badly. One of the points that caught his attention was the play of the second baseman—me—who was hitting about .240.

I guess Dyer did some fast talking, and convinced Breadon that I was just in a slump and would snap out of it. Maybe because he was worried about his own job security a little bit, Dyer used to try whatever method he could think of to get me to stop swinging at bad pitches. He knew that if I could just become more selective at the plate I could be a much better hitter, and also draw a lot more walks.

I knew he was right, and I wish I could have done it. It wasn't from a lack of trying, I can guarantee that.

Players didn't have nearly as much contact with the owner of the team back then as they do today. The only time we ever saw

Breadon was at contract time, when you went in to find out how much he was going to pay you for the next season. You went in—you didn't have an agent—and there was very little negotiating. The only player on the Cardinals then who had an agent was Musial, and that was because he also had some business deals on the side like endorsements and commercials.

The owners held all the cards back then, because if you weren't willing to take what they were offering you, they would find somebody else who would. There were so many good players in the minors, just waiting for a chance, they always could come up with a replacement and you would be out of luck. There wasn't free agency, or arbitration, or even a player's union to come to your rescue and back you up if you thought a club wasn't treating you fairly.

Marty Marion actually was the guy who had the idea to form the player's pension plan, and it came after the 1946 World Series when he didn't think we were getting enough money. Our winner's share was about $2,700 a man, and we knew the club had taken in a lot more than that. We all pooled some money and hired a lawyer, and got players from other teams involved, and that led to the start of the pension plan, which today provides incredible benefits to all the players.

One thing I learned about Marion in the 1946 season was that he was afraid to fly. We were playing in New York, and the trains weren't running because of a strike. We had to get to Cincinnati, and Leo Ward, the traveling secretary, didn't know what to do. He finally arranged for enough of us to fly to Cincinnati to play the game, and made other arrangements — taking a bus, I guess — for the rest of the team to get there, including Marion. It was the first time I ever flew and was the Cardinals' first flight, on an old DC-3. The only thing I could think about was just wanting to get to Cincinnati so we could play the game.

They had to hold up the start of the game for us to get there, and we had to land in Dayton because of bad weather. A police escort was waiting for us and we sped off. We all piled into different cabs, with Stan, Slaughter and Moore and I grabbing one together. We were racing down the highway when all of a sudden the cab's hood popped up. The cabbie pulled off the road and asked, "Who can drive?" Stan took over behind the wheel, and the cabbie got out and laid down across the hood to keep it shut so we could get to the ballpark. He rode the rest of the way laying across the top of that hood. Stan tried to catch up to the police escort, but they were so far ahead we couldn't make up the difference. We pulled into a service station, and that hood popped up and the cabbie went flying. He was really lucky he wasn't hurt.

We finally got to the park, dressed as quickly as we could, and went out to play. Ewell Blackwell was pitching for the Reds, and I think I got the only hit we had. We lost the game, 1-0.

Mary and I made plans to be married, and I wanted the wedding to be during the season so all of the players could attend. We picked a date, September 20, when the team was playing at home that night against the Cubs. We were married at St. Margaret's Church in the morning, then all of the wedding party came down to Sportsman's Park for the game, and Mr. Breadon let everybody use his box, right down by the dugout.

For some reason, Dyer had me playing third that day instead of my normal spot at second. It also was one of those days when the hitters kept ripping line drives right at me. One shot in particular almost took my head off. When Eddie ran into Mary later and congratulated her on the wedding, she thanked him and said, "Please get Red off third base before he gets killed." I didn't even get any hits that day.

The wedding was the definite highlight of my season. Mary went with me on the final road trip to Pittsburgh, Cincinnati and Chicago, and then we came home for the winter. We took a real honeymoon to the Lake of the Ozarks, accompanied by the Musials, and started our new life together.

Because she was such a fan of the game, Mary was always involved in trying to help me improve and always was concerned for me when things didn't go well. When I was struggling a little at the start of the 1948 season, Dyer decided to talk with Mary to see if she could do anything that would convince me to stop swinging at so many high pitches.

I didn't know the two of them had talked, and so I was surprised when I was ready to leave on the first road trip of the season and Mary told me, "Have a good trip honey, get some hits and don't swing at bad pitches."

I sat my suitcase down on the sidewalk and stared at her. "What did you say?" I questioned Mary. She repeated the advice, and then I asked her who she had been talking to—and I found out it was Eddie Dyer.

"If you lay off high pitches, Red, he says you'd be a .300 hitter," Mary told me.

I knew that Mary, Dyer and everybody else was right, but knowing something and being able to act on that knowledge are two different things. I see hitters today who have the same problem— higher pitches look easier to hit because they are closer to your eyes. Today, with the lower strike zone, you can take those pitches for balls. In my day, if you took it, it was a strike. I guess I just figured if it was going to be a strike anyway, I might as well swing.

I tried to heed my wife's advice, however, and that was one of the reasons my average did climb the longer I played. I got into a groove occasionally where it seemed everything I hit found a hole. You're happy when things go your way like that, but you know you also are going to have stretches when everything you hit well happens to be right at somebody and those periods can be very frustrating. In one three-game stretch, I hit eight doubles, a home run and a single—10 hits in 14 at-bats. A year later I went through a stretch of collecting 15 hits in 26 at-bats. In 1949 I just missed hitting .300 for the first time in my career, finishing at .297.

The other reason I was able to have a little more success hitting came about by accident. Playing golf one day in spring training, I made the discovery that if I used my wrists, I could drive the golf ball a lot farther. That made me realize I really had not been using my wrists correctly in my baseball swing, and if it worked in golf, why wouldn't it work in baseball? I made a conscious effort to snap my wrists more on my swing, and it provided good results.

My hitting also improved as I got older simply out of experience. A lot of people forgot that I was only 22 years old when I reached the major leagues and had spent less than two years in the minors. It was only natural that I was still learning and would get better the more comfortable I got with my own game and learned the instincts and habits of different pitchers.

I also spent so much time worrying about my defensive skills that it probably took a little away from my hitting. I had one string of playing 44 consecutive games at second base without an error — a streak that was snapped when I made two in two innings.

Red was always such an instinctive player. He always knew what he had to do. He learned a great deal from playing with all of those great players. Terry Moore and Marty Marion taught Red a lot. It didn't take him long. He always knew where he was supposed to be.
—Mary Schoendienst

Mary always was my biggest supporter, and after Breadon sold the club to Fred Saigh and Robert Hannegan, she thought I wasn't being treated fairly with their contract offer. She walked into Saigh's office and told him I was worth more money. When you look back on it, she really was the first woman agent. Mary always said I was not the kind of guy who could tell an owner I was worth more money, and she was right, so I let her do it for me.

I just told Mr. Saigh, "You are paying Stan Musial so much money, and don't you think Red is half the player Stan Musial is?" He agreed, and Red got the raise. I thought if Red will not speak up, I will speak up. Mr. Saigh's line to me was "I can give you a Cadillac but I can't give you a Rolls Royce." Red had never been recognized for all the things he did for the team. I thought it was time he got the recognition he deserved. He did not get the contract I was seeking, but it was a good contract.
—Mary Schoendienst

Mary did more for me than negotiate contracts and offer hitting advice. She was able to take care of the house and the kids, which normally should be a two-parent job. She did it all, and she did a wonderful job. When I look back on it, I don't know how she was able to do all of the things she did without much help from me. She jokes that she would tell me to do something around the house, but then a call would come with somebody inviting me to play golf or do something else, and off I went. She says I was never handy around the house, but that's not true. I do know how to change a light bulb.

One of the activities I enjoyed the most in those days was some barnstorming trips we used to make after the season. All of my brothers played, and Joe Linneman's brother would call around and line up games in Farmington, Cape Girardeau and other small towns in Missouri and Illinois. We had an entire infield made up of Schoendiensts. It probably was a good thing there weren't any radio broadcasts of those games, or fans would have been totally confused. We made a few bucks, but we mainly just had a good time all playing together.

It would have been more enjoyable had the Cardinals won another pennant, and we did come close in 1949. My season ended four days early—the first time I ever broke a bone in my body. Slaughter threw a ball in from left field to me at second, and it skipped off my thumb, chipping the bone. The trainer, Doc Weaver, thought it was just out of place and he pulled on it and said it was all right, but I couldn't throw. I had to come out of the game and also missed the final three games. We went to the final day with a chance to tie Brooklyn, but we lost and the Dodgers won and we came in second.

I didn't have a lot to be sorry or disappointed about, however. I had become a successful major-leaguer, I was happily married, and I thought there were going to be a lot more good times to come in the 1950s.

Chapter 5

BASEBALL, AND A FAMILY TOO

S hagging flies in the outfield with other members of the 1950 National League All-Star team at Comiskey Park in Chicago was the kind of moment you dream of as a little boy. We could just as easily have been playing in the backyard of a house in Germantown, talking about what we were going to do when we got in the game.

Dick Sisler, Duke Snider, Walker Cooper and some other guys all were kidding each other that we might not even get to play, so why should we worry about what we were going to do?

When it came my turn, I boldly declared, "I'm going to hit one right up there, in the upper deck," pointing to right field.

I don't know why I said that. It just came out. I wasn't a home run hitter, and the last thing I should be trying to do in an All-Star game is hit a home run.

The statement produced some laughter from the other assembled players, and Sisler and I even bet a Coke on who would hit the longest ball when we got in the game. When he got into the game in the sixth inning and produced a single, I thought I was going to have to pay up.

The game went into extra innings, however, and my turn to bat finally came in the 14th inning. Ted Gray, a lefthanded pitcher, was on the mound for the American League, which meant I was going to bat righthanded.

The players who had heard my pre-game boast didn't let me forget it. "You going to hit it up in the right-field stands?" Cooper asked. "No," I said, "Left field now."

Lo and behold, I did it—hitting a homer into the left-field stands on the first pitch. I don't know if the guys on the bench were as shocked as I was, but they didn't have to make it around the bases without falling down laughing. When I did make it back to the dugout, the guys let me have it.

"You kept your word," Cooper said.

All-Star games always were a lot of fun for me, but that game definitely was a career highlight. Only once did I go to the game and not get to play, in Philadelphia in 1952, and that was because the game was called after five innings because of rain, just as I was getting ready to go into the game.

Part of the reason players in those days seemed to enjoy the All-Star game more than players do today was because it was more of a rarity. Without television, you never got to see the stars from the other league. All you knew were the names in the boxscore, and it was a treat for me and the other National League players to watch the American Leaguers and get to meet them. Today you don't have that separation any more, and I think that has taken something away from the enjoyment and kind of mystical appeal the All-Star game used to have.

Nobody said they weren't going to go if they didn't get a bonus. Nobody got a bonus for making the All-Star team. You got a gift, something like a cigarette box or a tie tack or a watch, but that was it— except for the satisfaction of knowing you had been chosen as one of the best players in your league. That was good enough for us.

Players today have a different reaction to almost everything than the players did in the 1940s and 1950s, and the biggest reason, I think, is television. We are all different today because of television, whether you're an athlete or work in any other profession. It has changed everything about everyone's jobs, mostly for the better, sometimes for the worst. As I said, for all of the good television has brought to the game of baseball, the one thing I think it has taken away is the mystical aspect of the game. You can't lie in bed and listen to a radio broadcast from Fenway Park and imagine what the Green Monster looks like—you can see it on television.

You don't get to imagine how Ken Griffey swings when he turns on a fastball. It's there, every night, waiting for you on Sportscenter. It has made the country in general, and in particular the sports world, a much faster-paced, more highlight-oriented world. That lets us know more about what happened, and certainly gives us the information faster, but it has lost something in the process.

Baseball used to be a newspaper game. You had to wait until you picked up the morning newspaper to find out the scores of the other games from the previous day and night, looking at the standings to find out if you had gained ground or lost a game.

The influence of television has changed the way writers for newspapers cover baseball. It has put them into a different role, and has changed the relationship many players used to have with writers. They weren't the enemy to us, they were friends, and there wasn't the separation between the two sides that seems to exist today.

Many writers never even came to the clubhouse. They would sit in the press box and write their stories, and if they needed to talk to anybody, they would come down and question the manager and that was it. I know a lot of players today wish that would be the case now, but it can't be because of television. When I was playing, fans relied on the newspaper to give them the detailed information about the game, the nuts-and-bolts details of who won and why. Today, they get that information from television, so the newspapers have to deliver more. Stories have become more analytical and more opinionated, and that's why it has become easier to alienate the players.

If a writer wanted to talk to a specific player, he almost always set up the interview in advance, not just showing up at the player's locker and waiting for him. We used to have three newspapers in St. Louis—the *Post-Dispatch*, the *Globe-Democrat* and the *Star-Times*. There were never mobs of writers just hanging around the locker room, like now, and that was the case even when we went to Boston and New York, where they had lots of newspapers. You would see the writers on the field before the game, and that was usually about it.

Players back then always read the newspaper, and I believe most of them do today, even if they say they don't. How else are they going to know if somebody writes something bad about them?

Part of the reason for the close relationship between writers and players was the travel in those days. We always went by train, and the writers and players would have more time to mingle and talk. Writers could talk to players as friends, and not always be interviewing a guy for a story. It also was a big reason why I think teams in general were a lot more closely-knit than they are today. We spent so much time together, we had to become friends. We had no choice.

Leo Ward was our traveling secretary, and it was his job to take care of all the arrangements, booking the trains, seeing that we got to the station on time, etc. That was a tough job then, and it still is today. Most players would not have the foggiest idea about what to do to get from one place to another if the traveling secretary didn't do it for them.

Leo had a simple way of assigning berths. He went by uniform number, and if the player was a regular or a reserve. Regulars got a lower berth. The number 2 berth was right above the wheels. I used to always ask the porter on the train to make up the upper berth, because it was easier to sleep up there. We usually had two separate cars that were hooked on to the rest of a train, but they were private so no one could just come walking through.

We spent a lot of time on the train. Our longest trip was to Boston, and we usually would leave about 8 o'clock Sunday night after playing a doubleheader. We would travel all night and all day Monday, and get to Boston in time to play on Tuesday. We stayed there for three or four games, then we would go to New York and stay a week, playing both the Dodgers and Giants. Then sometimes we would make the rest of the circuit around the league, stopping in Philadelphia, Pittsburgh, Cincinnati and Chicago. We were gone for 24 days if we did that, playing in all seven opponents' cities. It made a 12-game trip seem short. We also enjoyed longer homestands than players do today, however, sometimes being home for 15 or 18 consecutive days.

We played games while riding the trains, pretty much any kind of card game you can name—hearts, cribbage, pinochle. The food was good, great steaks and breakfasts, but the problem was we usually didn't have enough money to eat the way we would have liked.

We were on a trip one time, in 1947, when Harry Walker was traded. We had been in the middle of game of pinochle, and he was ahead of Stan and me. We always played for nickels and pennies; you couldn't ever lose more than $2. Stan and I were both down about $2 when Harry was traded, and we had a rule that we always had to finish the game. We didn't ever get to finish it, even though we kidded Harry about it for a long time. I wonder if he still has that slip.

Not only were the train trips different than flying on airplanes today, players had to carry their own bags. We were responsible for getting our own bags and making sure they got on the train. Players today have somebody pick up their bags in their hotel room and never see them again or think about them until they are in the next city, in the next hotel, waiting for somebody to bring them to their room.

We also didn't have buses waiting for us when we arrived in a new city. We took cabs, at our own expense, and we always tried to pile as many guys as we could in a cab. We were no different than all of the other passengers getting off the train, trying to hail a cab.

Traveling in that manner had a lot to do with building the camaraderie on a team and making it a really closely-knit bunch of guys. We were with one another, we had no choice. We didn't have the kind of money players do today, which gives them the ability to go off by themselves and get away from the rest of the team. We didn't have that luxury.

I used to enjoy all of the cities we went to. Boston was one of my favorites, and it was a shame we didn't get to go there anymore after the Braves moved to Milwaukee. We stayed at the old Kenmore Hotel, which is now part of Boston University. It was very convenient, and there were some great restaurants there as well.

New York was great, because when we got there we stayed for a week, playing both the Dodgers and Giants. The cab drivers knew the celebrities and the ballplayers, and they knew how to get to where they were going. Now if you get into a cab in New York it's not automatic that you're going to get where you are going. The driver has to look in the book and see if he can find it, then he drives you around the block two or three times. There are cab drivers in New York who literally can't drive from Manhattan to Yankee Stadium. I couldn't do it, either, but it's not my job. If it was my job, I guarantee that I would learn the way.

New York was fun because of the diversity of the Polo Grounds and Ebbets Field. Ebbets Field was small, and there wasn't much room to catch foul balls. The bullpen catcher used to sit there with a towel, and if he could tell that a ball was going to hit the fence, he would pick up a towel and start waving it. That let the runners take off and get a quicker jump. The league made teams stop doing that.

The Polo Grounds was the opposite because it was so big. Left center field was huge, but right field was short, 250 feet down the line. Fifty yards away, it was about 340 feet. If you hit one down the line, you had to run like hell to get a double. We always stayed at the old Commodore Hotel, right next to Grand Central Station. It's now the Grand Hyatt, and teams still stay there. Today, however, they have air conditioning in the hotel.

Of all the so-called "modern" conveniences that have come along over the years, the best has been air conditioning. I really don't know what we did all of those years without it. Everybody is spoiled now, and if you go into a building in the summer that isn't air-conditioned, you think you're going to die. Maybe it wasn't as hot back then.

My favorite city was and is Chicago. There's no better city in the world. I love Chicago. It's a big city, but it's like a small town. I made a lot of friends there, went to a lot of exciting places, and spent many a night eating a great dinner at one restaurant after another. It's the best.

They kept playing all of the games during the day at Wrigley Field long after lights had gone up in every other park in baseball, which also was part of the charm and appeal of the park and the city. You had more time to go to dinner and enjoy everything it had to offer.

Saying that, however, doesn't change the fact that I really preferred night games to day games. Once they improved the lights, I honestly believe I could see the ball better at night when I was hitting. It may have had something to do with my old eye injury, but I didn't see shadows on the ball when we played at night, and I always found it easier to pick up the ball. Some people may not agree with that, but that's the way it was for me.

The other advantage to night baseball was that it was cooler, which made a big difference because of the uniforms. They weren't the lightweight fabric that we have today. They were the heavy, woolen material, and when it was hot and you started to sweat, they weighed a ton. Those uniforms just hung on you, and if you were sweating, you had to pull on them in order to breathe a little. We got by, because we didn't know any better. Some of the most amazing records from the early days to me are the stolen base numbers, because guys had to be really fast and really strong to lug those heavy uniforms and still be able to steal a base.

We tried to battle the heat with salt pills. The trainer would leave them out on top of the water cooler and you would take a salt pill in between every inning. Now they tell you salt is bad for you. We didn't know that back then. Then again, it seems almost everything is bad for you now for one reason or another. It was a simpler time when we didn't know all that stuff.

Television has helped to educate a lot of the people about medical concerns and other areas, but another influence has been in baseball, where I really believe it has affected the strike zone. Umpires will say it isn't true, but they do have a smaller zone than when I played. Umpires are worried that if they call a pitch a strike and the television replays show it was just a little inside or outside, or high or low, that people will use that to criticize them. A pitch almost has to be right down the middle, belt high, to be called a strike anymore.

The squeezing of the strike zone has made it a lot harder to be a pitcher today. Pitchers in my day generally used one strategy, high and inside, low and away. I still believe it's the best way to pitch. Pitchers spent more time in the minor leagues, learning how to pitch, and they used that knowledge when they got to the majors. They would look for weaknesses in hitters, and coaches would watch batting practice and give the pitcher little tips they could try to use on hitters.

My weakness was the high fastball. Pitchers knew I had a tendency to go after high pitches, so they would usually start out throwing strikes then keep inching the ball up a little higher and higher, hoping I would swing at them. The pitchers who could put some movement on their fastball really were tough to hit.

A lot of the Dodger pitchers gave me trouble—Sandy Koufax and Carl Erskine in particular. I didn't have much luck against Johnny Podres, either. I wasn't the only one who had trouble against those guys. They knew how to pitch and they had great stuff. If you got a loud foul ball off of them you almost considered it a moral victory.

Pitchers used to throw more strikes, and that was because of the bigger strike zone. Ballgames used to last two hours, and that was the reason. You didn't have to have a two-minute break between innings because of television. Some of the rules on balk moves were different, and that meant pitchers didn't spend so much time making unnecessary throws to first base.

When you win a game, you don't care how long it lasts. It generally seems like a shorter game when you win, and when your team is successful and winning a lot, the season goes by very quickly. On the other hand, if you are losing the majority of your games, the season can seem like it lasts forever.

Unfortunately, that is the pattern the Cardinals found themselves in in the early 1950s. In the six seasons from 1950 through 1955, we didn't finish higher than third, even in 1952, when we won 88 games and were 22 games above .500.

Changing managers didn't help. We went from Eddie Dyer to Marty Marion to Eddie Stanky without the situation changing. Making trades didn't help. Joe Garagiola went to Pittsburgh and Enos Slaughter went to the Yankees, and still we lost.

We even changed owners. Fred Saigh ran into trouble with the government, being charged with income tax evasion, and was forced to sell the team. It looked for a while like no one in St. Louis was going to step forward and buy the club and we might be sold to a group in Milwaukee, which would have moved the team there, but then August Busch Jr. and Anheuser-Busch stepped forward.

Mr. Busch was not a big baseball fan, but he was a smart businessman, and he was one of the leading promoters of St. Louis. He knew having the Cardinals in St. Louis was good for the community, and he was enough of a sportsman that once he bought the club and became involved in its operations, he become hooked.

About a year before Busch bought the Cardinals, he had Stan and I and Leo Ward out to his hunting lodge for lunch. I had met him before, but had not really gotten to know him. We were talking about the ballclub, and what was going to happen to the franchise, and both Stan and I suggested that Busch buy the team. His response was that he didn't know much about baseball, but I wonder if he already had been thinking about it and just wanted to see what our reaction would be.

He was a fun owner. He wanted to win, and losses really upset him. He ran the baseball team the way he ran the brewery. There was only one way to do something, his way, and it had to be done correctly. If it wasn't going to be done the right way, then don't do it.

He spent a lot of time around the ballclub in those early days, putting on a uniform and taking batting practice during spring training and posing for lots of pictures. He often said he got more attention and publicity from owning the Cardinals than he did for running Anheuser-Busch, a much larger and more worldly corporation.

He went to every ballgame at home, and he even had his own private railroad car that he hooked onto our cars when we took off on road trips and he went with us. At home, he had his "roost" up near the top of the stadium, and he would sit there with his friends and watch the game. Now, some people would probably say he was a meddlesome owner and that he got too involved in the team's day-to-day activities, but I think it was because he was so excited to be involved with the team and just wanted to be in the know about what was going on.

No matter what he was doing, Busch wanted to win, whether it was playing cards, in baseball, in business, whatever. He'd try to find out how he could win, what it would take, would surround himself with the people he thought could do the job and if they didn't, he demanded answers and explanations. I honestly believe he thought winning in baseball was going to be easy, but it didn't turn out that way. He thought he could just go out and acquire the players he needed to make the Cardinals better, but he found out other owners were just as powerful as he was. Phil Wrigley of the Cubs wasn't willing to sell Ernie Banks to Busch, and neither was Horace Stoneham of the Giants willing to part with Willie Mays, no matter how much money Busch was offering. That was different than the business world Busch had come from, and it took him time to adjust to that.

We became good friends, and I always viewed Mr. Busch as someone who appreciated honesty, loyalty and friendship. He expected and demanded a lot from his workers, but he also treated them well. He tried to surround himself with good people who knew what they were doing, and he had faith in their opinions and judgments.

It just happened that Mr. Busch's first year of owning the Cardinals, 1953, turned out to be the best statistical season of my career. I was locked in a battle for the league batting title with Carl Furillo of the Dodgers, when for some reason, fans from my hometown in Clinton County, Illinois, and people in St. Louis decided to have a night and honor me before a game at Busch Stadium.

It wasn't something I asked for and I certainly wasn't retiring, but they decided to do it anyway, and Mary and I were very appreciative. We received a wide range of gifts, everything from a Lincoln Capri convertible to a basket of peaches. Mr. Busch gave me a new shotgun; Mary gave me a gun rack; the people in Germantown gave me a new hunting dog; a St. Louis company gave me a new vacuum cleaner and my teammates pooled their money and bought us an engraved eight-piece set of Bavarian china. With funds left over from the purchase of the car, we also received a new deep freeze and a 21-inch television.

The night really overwhelmed me, and made me think they wanted me to retire. I then went out and got three hits against the Cubs, a single, double and triple, so I decided to keep playing.

The fans in St. Louis always were great to me, and Mary got a revealing lesson in the power of baseball one day when she was asked to come visit the boys at St. Joseph's school and talk to them.

As I was leaving, one boy came up to me and handed me a Cardinal bird figurine. "I want you to have this," he said. I thanked him, because it was beautiful. Afterward, one of the Sisters said to me, "Mary, that is the first time that boy has ever spoken." I was really honored that he cared that much about my coming to the school. I have collected a lot of Cardinal figurines since that day, but that one has remained one of the most special pieces of my collection.

— Mary Schoendienst

A player can't worry about the fans when he's playing, and you really can't think about anything not connected with winning or losing a game, like a batting race. It was hard not to think about the batting race, considering it was a new experience for me. I had finally reached the .300 mark by finishing at .303 in 1952, but that was still 33 percentage points behind my roommate. Stan led the league that year with a .336 average.

Going into September of 1953, however, I saw where I really had a chance to win the title and that gave me a little more incentive to go out and play well then I might have normally had with the team out of the race. Playing games in September is tough—players are tired, and if you are in a pennant race, there is pressure bearing down on you every day during every game. Good ballplayers play at a certain level all of the time, but still they tend to rise to the challenge of playing their best during important games.

I would have been a little fresher and had a little more success had I had more rest that year. The only days I didn't play all year were because of a variety of injuries, including pulled ankle ligaments and a torn abdominal muscle. The worst injury I suffered that year came in New York, against the Giants, when an errant throw by Alvin Dark caught me just above my left eye as I was crossing first base. Doctors at first were worried that I had suffered an injury to my eye, but that was before we were able to tell them about the injury in the CCC camp.

Still, I suffered severe headaches and fuzzy vision and spent several days in the hospital for tests when the team returned to St. Louis. The doctor thought I should miss even more games, but I wanted to get back to the team. The first day after I rejoined the team, I came off the bench to pinch-hit against Pittsburgh and managed to smack a double, driving in two runs. I was back in the starting lineup the next day.

With three weeks to go in the season, I caught a bad break—a broken hand. It wasn't my hand that was broken, it was Furillo's, and that meant he would miss the rest of the season and his average was frozen at .344. Stan was having an off-year, for him, and that's what set the stage for me to battle it out with Furillo for the title.

If Furillo had played those last three weeks, I believe I would have won the title. It's hard to maintain a high average in September, and if he had struggled at all, his average would have dropped. Instead it remained the same, and I knew the target I had to shoot at.

When Furillo went down—injured in a brawl between the Dodgers and Giants—I was hitting .339. With one week to go in the season, my average had dropped to .333, and suddenly I found myself fourth in the race, trailing not only Furillo but Duke Snider of the Dodgers and Don Mueller of the Giants as well. Three good days—3-for-3, 4-for-7 and 3-for-4, lifted my average back to .339 as we prepared to play the Cubs the last four games of the season, in Chicago.

A week or so earlier, Hank Sauer of the Cubs and I had bumped into each other when both teams were playing in New York. He told me, "Red, I hope you win it."

My manager, Eddie Stanky, really wanted me to win the title. He was upset that Furillo was going to win without having to play the last three weeks, and he told me if I could just get ahead of him, he would pull me out of the lineup and let me set out the rest of the year so I could win it.

"No Eddie," I told him at the time. "I don't want to win that way. I want to keep playing."

I had some brief thoughts that Eddie and I might get into a fight about it. In the opening doubleheader against the Cubs, I collected four hits and raised my average to .343, one point behind Furillo, with two games to go.

In my first at-bat in the next game, I singled. The next time up, I hit a wicked line drive to right that Sauer somehow managed to catch, robbing me of a hit. I was retired in my next two at-bats, and went into the final day of the year still at .343, one point behind Furillo.

I was determined to do the best I could and just see what happened. Hits in my first two at-bats gave me a chance, and after Stanky conferred with the people in the press box and determined I still was a fraction of a point behind Furillo, I went up to bat again and like the day before, hit a ball toward Sauer in right field.

Like the day before, Sauer again managed to make the catch. If he had missed either that ball or the one on the previous day, I would have edged out Furillo. It just wasn't meant to be, and Sauer's comment that he hoped I would win —and that he was the one who robbed me with those two catches— made for an incredible piece of irony.

One more hit, anywhere over the course of the season, and I would have won the title. When you come that close, you would have liked to have won it.

I was at home, listening to the game on the radio. Father Cronin spent the game walking in front of our house, and I know he was praying that Red would get the hits. I called out to him, "He's got two. he needs one more." Hank Sauer made the plays, and Red didn't get the hit. The Cubs weren't going to give the title to Red. Sauer wanted Red to win it, but he wanted him to do it on his own and earn it.

— Mary Schoendienst

Mary probably worried more about what my reaction would be to losing out on the batting title than I did. I made no secret of the fact I would have liked to have won it, but I didn't, it was over, and there wasn't anything I was going to do about it. My nature wasn't, and isn't now, to worry about too many things I can't control. If that makes me a simple, happy-go-lucky kind of guy, I guess that's just the way it is.

Mary always worried more about me than I did. She worried what would happen to me if I got hurt, but I always figured I would get well. If my arm hurt too badly to throw, I would move to first base or learn to throw lefthanded. She always was concerned because I had a habit of taking my glove off in between every pitch. I don't know why I did it, except maybe because during the hot summer days I would get some sweat on my hand and I was able to wipe it off when I took my glove off.

I always got my glove back on before the pitch, but Mary was worried that one day I wouldn't make it in time and would mess up a play. I never worried about that, but then I was never nervous when I played. I wanted the ball hit to me.

I'm certain there were players who were nervous and didn't want the ball hit to them, but I never heard anybody admit it. Players in my era also never complained when the manager told them to do something they didn't necessarily want to do. An example was that since I was usually the No. 2 hitter in the batting order, it was my job on numerous occasions to give myself up, hitting a ball to the right side, simply to move the runner up to second base. The out, of course, affected my batting average but many times helped produce a victory, which really was all everybody worried about back then. We didn't have to go before an arbitrator in the off-season, who didn't care about anything except the raw numbers and would rule that 200 hits was worth a lot more money than 180 hits, no matter how many games the team won.

If I was playing now, I'm certain I would worry more about money than I ever did in my career. Mary was always concerned about whether we could afford whatever it was we were buying, and that was the case once when she told me she really would like a fur coat.

I told her fine, I would get her one, but she wanted to know how we would pay for it. I joked that I was going to get her a fur coat, but what Mary didn't know was that I was going to get a few traps out so she could trap the minks herself.

I kept bugging him about it, and he kept telling me not to worry about it. He said he was going to win the batting title the next year and that would pay for it. I got the coat, but Red didn't win the title. We still paid for the coat.
— Mary Schoendienst

As much fun as it had been to be in the race for the batting title, the fact the Cardinals hadn't won as a team for a few years was frustrating, and I know it was the biggest reason behind the shocking trade of Enos Slaughter to the Yankees just before the 1954 season began.

Fans were outraged by the deal, and some even canceled their season tickets. As players, you always know that anybody can be traded at any time, but there are still deals that sometimes surprise you. This was one of them, and left everybody in that clubhouse thinking they could be the next one to go.

Enos was very disappointed, but he went to a good ballclub with an excellent chance to win and they did win. He played the same way in New York as he had played in St. Louis, because that was the only way he knew how to play.

Some guys only put out when they know the boss is watching or the camera is running, but not Enos. It wasn't a put-on with him. Whatever it took, he was going to win. He played hard all the time.

Some people thought Enos was a "dirty" player, but I never saw any sign of that. What I saw was a guy who didn't want to hurt anybody, but if he had to take a guy out at second base to break up a double play, that's exactly what he did. He slid hard and he played hard. Guys like him and Terry Moore were great to have on your ballclub, because when they played like that it made everybody else play hard as well. They would let you know if they didn't think you were playing hard enough.

There were guys like that on every team in the league. When you went into Brooklyn or to play the Giants or just about anybody else, you knew they were going to be playing hard. You had to play hard against them if you were going to have any chance to win. It isn't that way so much today, but the biggest reason has nothing to do with the players—it's the change in the rules that has made it a different game.

You can't slide the same way or take a guy out at second or you will be called out for interference. The rules today protect the players a lot more than in the 1950s, when the only protection you had came from yourself and your teammates.

There are still a lot of great players today, but there were more back then, because teams had so many more players to chose from, and there were only eight teams in each league. The Cardinals alone had 25 or 30 farm teams. If you had to find a replacement for an injured player, there always was a very good player waiting for his chance. Now if a guy gets hurt, sometimes it's a real struggle to find somebody to call up and take his place, and often it's a guy who isn't ready for the majors but is the only choice you've got.

Part of the reason guys don't seem to play as hard today as they did 40 and 50 years ago is the same reason—there isn't anybody ready who can take their place. Then, you either played hard all the time or they would find somebody else who would.

The job of replacing Enos fell to rookie Wally Moon, and he was ready. He went on to become the NL Rookie of the Year in 1954, the same year the Cardinals became an integrated team when Tom Alston, a tall gangly first baseman, joined the team. He wasn't ready for the majors.

Mr. Busch knew the Cardinals needed to have black players, and some scout had recommended Alston, but he just didn't have the experience he needed to play at the major-league level. He was a good guy, and he worked hard and tried to learn everything possible, but the ability just wasn't there.

Guys like Durocher were especially hard on him, but Durocher was hard on every rookie. That was part of the way he decided if a guy was a major leaguer or not by the way he handled his rookie initiation. Another guy Durocher always seemed to be riding was Dick Sisler, who also played first base in the 1940s and 1950s.

Durocher just wouldn't let up on Sisler, who had a stuttering problem. He called Sisler all kinds of names, and one time just as Sisler made the third out in the field, Durocher called him "a big water buffalo."

I'll never forget Dick calling on the phone one day, and after I said hello, he said, "Doooo youuuu knowwww whoooo thissss isssss?" I couldn't keep myself from laughing out loud.

Dick was a smart, well-educated guy. He never played as well as he or the Cardinals expected, and I know he was disappointed because of that. He still was a popular player, and he and a bunch of other major-leaguers used to barnstorm through the south during the winter. One time, he was driving a van and had to stop for gas. He had to go to the restroom, so he hopped out of the van and yelled to the attendant, "Filllll ittttttt uppppp."

What neither Dick nor anybody else knew, however, was that the gas station attendant also was a stutterer. He looked at Dick and said, "Youuuuu aaaaaa wissseeeee guyyyyy?"

This was in the day when players used to leave their gloves on the field when they went in to bat. That was one tradition I never really understood, but more amazing is the fact that in all the years players left their gloves on the field while they were hitting, I never saw a ball hit one of those gloves, and I never saw a defensive player trip over one of those gloves. I do remember the bats being lined up on the ground outside the dugout, and guys stumbling over them as they tried to catch a foul ball, before they changed that rule and put the bats in the dugout.

Anyway, Sisler was so rattled by Durocher that day and being called a water buffalo, that after he caught the ball, he rolled the ball to the coaching box where he ordinarily left his glove and dropped his glove on the pitching mound. Leo's ranting and raving had Sisler all messed up.

One thing everybody who played with the Cardinals in those days had to tolerate was playing at Sportsman's Park, which was renamed Busch Stadium after Mr. Busch bought the team. The park was in bad shape, mainly because it was old, and Mr. Busch tried to do what he could to fix it up but there was only so much he could do, and that's why he finally spearheaded the effort to build the new stadium downtown. The changes he tried to put in place at the old park were mainly for the comfort of the fans, like improving the bathrooms. There wasn't much he could do on the field, where the infield was rough.

Part of the reason, of course, was up until the Browns moved to Baltimore you had two teams sharing the same field. One team was home virtually every day from April through September. The grounds crew didn't get time to work on the field when one of the teams was out of town, because the other was home. It rained a lot in the spring, and the grass would be really heavy. It was hard to hit a ball past the infield because the grass was so high. There were a lot of times when we found rocks in the infield.

After all the rain, the sun would come out and bake the infield as hard as a rock. There were guys who slid into bases, and actually had their pants torn by a rock.

It was kind of a strange ballpark, but it had a lot of character. Right field was shallow, but it had a huge screen. If you hit a line drive, you had to run like hell to get a double. Guys had to learn to play the ball off the screen because it never bounced off there with a true hop. It would always go to the right or the left. The opposite was true in left field and left center, where the dimensions were huge.

One question that will never be answered was what kind of hitter I would have been had I not suffered the eye injury in the CCC camp. My left eye always bothered me, and it even reached the point in 1955 where Dr. Middleman wanted me to wear glasses. He fitted me for them, and I tried them—for a week.

I really didn't think they were helping me see any better, and I didn't feel comfortable wearing them. I forgot them in my locker one day, and went out and got three hits against Warren Spahn. I said, "Well, that's the end of that." I do wear glasses now when I read—Walgreens specials, $9.95.

My eyesight was good enough to see that the team was struggling, and Eddie Stanky was fired as manager in 1955 and replaced by my old teammate, Harry Walker. Stanky had been a good manager and he knew the game and I was sorry when he got fired. I can honestly say I liked every manager I played for because I just did what I had to do. I didn't interfere with anything, I just went out and did my business and they usually left me alone. All Eddie asked was that you work hard, and if you did, he never bothered you.

The only time a manager and I ever exchanged harsh words was one time when Eddie Dyer was running the club. He gave all the signs, and one time I took off from first and stole second even though he had not given me the steal sign. Musial was batting after me.

After the game, Dyer called me into his office and said, "You steal a base when I tell you to steal a base." I should have said, "Yes, sir" and let it go at that, but I tried to defend myself. "I thought I could make it and I did," I argued. "I stole it easy."

That made Dyer mad. He said, "I want to tell you something. I'm running this ballclub." I agreed with him that time, but he continued, "When I tell you to steal, you steal. When you don't get the sign, stay at first base. You've got Musial hitting after you, you can go from first base to third as well as anybody playing ball today. I want you there to keep that hole open for Musial, then we'll have first and third rather than you on second base and they'll pitch around Musial."

I knew I wasn't going to win the argument, so I just agreed and walked out of his office. I didn't steal a base on my own the rest of the year.

Managers were more respected when I played than they are today. He ran the ballclub, and you really couldn't ever disagree with him and not be punished for it. They had players waiting to take your place, and if you made the manager or the general manager unhappy, they wouldn't think twice about trading you or calling somebody up from the minors to take your place. Contracts were not a factor since almost everybody worked on a one-year deal, so it wasn't like moving you was going to cost the club a lot of money. There are plenty of times today when clubs would like to get rid of a player but they can't because it would mean having to eat millions of dollars, and they don't have the ability to do that.

Walker finished the 1955 season as the manager, and I think would have been allowed to continue the next year had Bing Devine become the Cardinals general manager. Instead, Mr. Busch went outside the organization and hired Frank Lane. He wanted his own manager, and brought in Fred Hutchinson.

Lane was a good politician. I can remember him sitting on the bench in spring training, and he was having trouble seeing well in those days. Reporters would come up to talk to him, and he was smart enough not to let one know that he couldn't see very well. We would be taking batting practice, and he'd hear the crack of the bat and say things like, "There's a fine ballplayer." He had no idea who was batting, but he was able to get away with statements like that.

Lane also had guts, but he never understood how important baseball tradition was in St. Louis. He changed the uniforms, and he did the unthinkable—suggest trading Musial to Philadelphia for Robin Roberts.

One day I picked Stan up on the way to the ballpark like I always did, and he was upset. I asked him what was wrong, and he said, "I think I'm going to be traded and I'm not going to go." I thought to myself, "Well, I imagine I'll be traded soon."

The team hadn't won in a while, and some of us were getting older. I knew they wanted to bring in some younger players, and that would require trading some of the older guys. I never heard any specific rumors, but I still kind of prepared myself for the news.

What made me mad, however, was how I found out I had been traded to the Giants—I heard it on the radio. I guess Lane's secretary tried to call after I already had left for the ballpark, but I didn't appreciate getting the news that way.

> *I was shocked. The secretary called and said, "Mary, I have very sad news for you. Red has just been traded to New York." I just about fell over. I sat down on the couch in the living room. I couldn't believe it. It was very hard. Back then, teams didn't trade major players. It didn't happen like it does today, and that made it hard to take.*
> — *Mary Schoendienst*

Having played in the Cardinals' system for 13 years also made the deal tougher to take. Stan says it was his saddest day in baseball. I thought I could still play, and I didn't want to have to uproot Mary and the rest of the family and move to New York. St. Louis was home, and that's where we wanted to be.

The trade also bothered me because as a fan of the Cardinals, I didn't think it was an equal trade. It was an eight-player deal, and the Cardinals also sent young outfielder Jackie Brandt to the Giants and the best player St. Louis received in return was shortstop Alvin Dark. I knew young second baseman Don Blasingame was going to take over for me, but I thought trading Brandt was a mistake. Brandt never turned out to be the kind of player I thought he would be, but I still thought trading him was a mistake.

I wrote a letter to the editors of the newspapers, thanking the fans for their support of Red. They put it in the papers. The people who were the most upset were the residents of Germantown, Red's home town. They had put up a sign as you entered town that said "Welcome to Germantown, home of Red Schoendienst, St. Louis Cardinals." They never changed the sign. The people there still thought of him as a Cardinal.

— Mary Schoendienst

I don't know if Mr. Busch ever regretted hiring Lane, but he didn't last long. He was gone at the end of the 1957 season, moving on to Cleveland. That finally gave Busch the opening to go ahead and give the job to Bing Devine.

Lane always amazed me by the way he tried to get close to players on the opposing teams. I remember in 1967 he was working for another team, and we were on a road trip. Musial was there, because that was the year he worked as general manager. He and I got on the team bus to go from the hotel to the ballpark. As soon as we sat down, I heard a voice coming from the seats a couple of rows behind us. I knew the voice sounded familiar, but I couldn't place it immediately. Then it came to me— it was Frank Lane. He was on our bus. He was talking to a couple of our players, trying to get a ride to the ballpark.

I never saw Stan move so fast in my life. He sprang up from his seat and walked to where Lane was sitting. "Get the hell out of here," he ordered Lane. "Get off our bus."

I wish Stan, or somebody else, had the authority to tell Lane what to do in earlier times. Then maybe I wouldn't have been headed to New York, becoming a member of the Giants.

Chapter 6

A Giant, a Brave, and Another World Series

Part of the reason the trade upset me was that I didn't know what effect it was going to have on my family. Mary and I had two daughters by then, Colleen and Cathleen, and I wanted to keep the family together and have them with me but I also knew it would be much harder on Mary to care for the girls by herself in a strange city without the help of her parents.

Mary, even though she was devastated by the trade, told me just to worry about playing baseball and she would take care of everything else. Leaving them and heading off to join the Giants in New York was a difficult thing to do, but I knew I had no other choice.

When I joined the Giants, my right arm was sore and prevented me from playing in the field. I was sitting on the bench watching the game in the seventh inning, when manager Bill Rigney needed a pinch-hitter and motioned for me to grab a bat.

Johnny Klippstein was pitching for the Reds, and I was able to come through with a two-run homer that tied the game. We went on to win 4-3 in 11 innings, a nice way for me to break in with the new team.

> *I had stayed in St. Louis, and was listening to the Cardinals game on the radio. Harry Caray was talking about Red and saying how sorry he was that Red had been traded. They went to a commercial or something, and all of a sudden Harry came back on all excited said, "Well, guess who just hit a home run for New York?" It was Red. I just said to myself, "He's just proving he's still capable of being a good player."*
>
> — *Mary Schoendienst*

The worst part about the trade, other than being separated from Mary and the kids, was that the Giants were not a good team. We finished the year in sixth place, out of eight teams, and were 26 games behind the first-place and cross-town rival Dodgers.

We had one pretty good player—Willie Mays, by then in his fifth full major-league season. He was one of those gifted players who did everything so effortlessly that it didn't appear he was trying or giving his best. The game came so easily and naturally for him—all phases from hitting to running and fielding—that his talent and performance were sometimes taken for granted. He ended up becoming one of the greatest players in the history of the game.

Playing second base in New York, and having been recognized as an All-Star a few times, set up a natural comparison between myself and Jackie Robinson, the second baseman for the Dodgers. I never made the comparisons, but others did, even though I tried not to pay much attention to that kind of stuff.

He was a good athlete and a good ballplayer. He probably could have gone out and played polo and done well. He certainly had done well in other sports before concentrating on baseball, including football, basketball and track and field. He also was playing on a good team, with a lot of good players surrounding him, and that always makes a difference as well.

Still, most of the attention Robinson received, especially early in his career, was because he had become the first black player in the major leagues. Some people got more worked up about that than I did, and I never really had much of an opinion one way or the other. Robinson was a good player, he obviously belonged in the major leagues, and whether he was white or black didn't bother me one bit. Some players on some teams didn't like the fact Robinson and Branch Rickey had integrated the major leagues, but I think those guys were in the minority. There were always rumors that players on the Cardinals were going to go on strike and not play against Robinson, but nobody ever said anything to me about it and I never saw any incidents that I thought were direct attempts to injure or harm Robinson.

Robinson had a good idea how to play, and the fact he was able to play as well as he did I'm certain opened the door to the majors for other black players more quickly than would have been the case had he failed. It didn't bother me that he got the extra attention, although his presence cost me a few starting assignments in All-Star games. I never sat down and analyzed how Jackie and I compared as players, knowing that all I concerned myself with was how I was performing and whether I was doing the job my team and my team-mates expected of me and needed from me for us to win.

It turned out that my only season in New York was the final year of Jackie's career as he retired after the 1956 season. Jackie and I never really had much direct contact or conversation, except for one day a few years after he had gotten out of the game. He was working for the Chock Full O' Nuts coffee company in Manhattan, and he just happened to come out of the office building on Lexington Ave. at the same time Del Rice and I were walking by, on our way to get something to eat.

I said, "Hi Jackie, how are you?" He acknowledged my greeting, and I asked if he missed the game. The question may have caught him a little off-guard, but he looked directly at me and his honest-to-God answer was, "Not one bit, Red." The light at the crosswalk changed, and we went our separate ways. That was the extent of our conversation.

Everybody says that when you play in New York you get more attention, and there is some merit to that. What limited the attention for the players on the Giants, however, was that we were not that potent a ballclub at the time, and with the Dodgers and Yankees playing each other in the World Series four times in a five-year span, we definitely were the third-rated club when it came to dividing up the space in the newspaper. My cause for individual attention also was hurt by a couple of factors—my sore arm, which really limited my playing time and affected my performance when I did play— and the fact that I didn't go out of my way seeking publicity like a lot of players. I made 10 All-Star teams, and I probably should have made more, but I don't have any room to complain. That never has been my style.

I did get involved in one public relations episode while I was playing for the Giants. The people in charge of the Arthur Murray dance contest called the Dodgers and Giants and asked them to send several players to enter the contest. The Dodgers had Carl Erskine and Duke Snider, the Giants had Sal Maglie and me.

We were supposed to dance with somebody in a competition. I didn't want to do it and neither did any of the other players. There was a cash prize involved, $1,000, and we all got together and said we were going to split the money up no matter who won. Well I ended up winning the first couple of rounds, and that meant I had to go back for the finals.

I was going up against the Harvest Moon dancers, professionals from New York. I had to dance with a different partner, and we lost. My consolation prize was $500, and I called Mary and asked her what I should give the girl who had been my partner.

She told me, "Give her your autograph and get out of there."

Another night I was being interviewed on a talk show and the host asked me to name my favorite song. Mary and I really enjoyed going to all the Broadway shows when we were in New York, like *The Desert Song*, and all these great classical numbers went through my mind, but the song that came out of my mouth was "Doodledy doo." The host wanted to play the song, and I didn't think he'd do it, but then he went on the air and said Schoendienst's favorite song was "Doodledy doo."

I just about died. Doodledy doo. I had taken him to the opera to see all those wonderful shows. He enjoyed

them. I was so embarrassed. I have taught the man good
music and he tells them he wants to play "Doodledy doo."
How do you figure the man out?

— *Mary Schoendienst*

I don't know if Jackie Robinson ever went on the radio with anybody and said what his favorite song was, but he received a lot of his attention because of his appearances in the World Series. That's really about the only time any player gets national attention, even today, unless you're somebody like Mark McGwire or Ken Griffey Jr. and are shooting for the home run record. People still remember players and specific plays from the World Series for a long time, where if the same player had made the same play during the regular season it probably would be forgotten.

Most of the players I knew and played with didn't really care about publicity, anyway. Almost all of them thought they weren't making enough money—similar to today—but they were happy just to play and if they were good enough, they knew they would get the respect they deserved from their fellow players. That's all they really cared about.

The attitude of the players was different in another way too. Today, a lot of the players act like they walk on water because they have the unique skill of being able to hit a baseball. When I played, we really didn't think we were that special. We thought we were lucky. Nobody I knew would come up to the traveling secretary and start making demands: "I want this" or "I want that." It was more the traveling secretary who said, "That's your room, take it." They put up a sign about what time the game was, what time the train was leaving after the game, and you had better be there. You could always be replaced, and every player was definitely aware of that possibility. A lot of today's players think they are invincible.

The arrival of spring training in 1957 brought about another change for me. The Giants' spring base was in Mesa, Arizona, so for the first time other than the war year when spring training was in Cairo, Illinois, I didn't pack my bags and head to Florida. I headed for Arizona, and Mary couldn't go because she was about to give birth to our third child.

I got the word that Mary was about to have the baby, so I hustled back to St. Louis. It was the only time I had been out of town when Mary was ready to deliver the baby, even though we almost missed connections when Colleen, our oldest daughter, was born. I didn't think Mary was that close to having the baby, and I had left her at home to go out and get the brakes fixed on the car. The doctor finally found me, and I got to the hospital on time.

Before I left Arizona to come home for a few days to be with Mary and our new daughter, Eileen, Jocko Conlon, the umpire, had been telling me about how cheap land was out there and that I really should look into investing in some land near the Buckhorn Ranch. We had some spots picked out that I was going to see with a real estate agent, but then I left to go home and when I got back into Phoenix a few days later, I was busy and forgot about it and never did go see the land. Talk about another missed opportunity. That land would be worth a fortune now.

After the trade the previous year, Dick Littlefield, a young pitcher who also was in the trade, and I had spent the rest of the season rooming together at the Mayfair Hotel at Columbus Square. This time, I really wanted Mary and the kids to come to stay with me in New York, so we rented a house in Hastings-on-the-Hudson, and it was a lovely place. The only problem was we had to pay the rent for the entire season up front, and Mary had been hesitant to OK the deal, wanting to make certain we would be there for the entire season. I told her I had no control over that, we just would hope for the best. She and the girls had been there only a few days when the Giants' owner, Horace Stoneham, surprised me with a telephone call late at night, close to midnight.

I had been traded again, exactly a year after the deal that had brought me to the Giants. This time, I was lucky. I was going to the Milwaukee Braves and Bobby Thomson was coming back to New York. I learned later the Cubs also had inquired about me, and I was glad that deal had not materialized.

Horace Stoneham was a great owner, primarily because he was such a good human being. Baseball was his business and he surrounded himself with good baseball people who knew and understood the game, from the general manager to the manager to the coaches and players. He and I stayed in contact even after the Giants moved to San Francisco. He would have me up in his office, and we would talk about all kinds of things. He cared about his players and their families and that was what made him such a good owner. There aren't many guys like him left in the game anymore, guys who run the baseball team as their only business, and that's a shame.

I had heard a lot of great things about playing in Milwaukee, how they had great fans and the ownership did a lot for the players. I knew it was going to be a better situation for me, because the team was better with a good chance to win, but the trade meant another move for Mary and the kids and I hated to put them through that again.

Red was really worried about me and I said, "Oh don't worry about me. I'll be fine. I didn't have any idea where I was or what was going on. I just said, "You go and play that game. They need you, Red or they would not have traded for you. I think he got three hits that day. I thought, "Now he's got his mind on track about what he is supposed to be doing, and now I've got to get mine on track."
— Mary Schoendienst

When fans see a transaction in the newspaper or hear about a trade on the radio, they realize the player has to pick up and move to a new city, but they sometimes don't realize the effect it has on a player's family as well. I was already playing for the Braves, and Mary was still in New York—her home for only a few days—and she had to figure out how to get the family on a plane to Milwaukee. She didn't even know where the airport was, or how to get there.

I had a cousin staying with me who lived in Queens. She didn't drive, but she brought her son along so he could drive back home. I had the two girls in the front seat, she was holding the baby in the back seat. When we got to the airport I let them out, and then I had to find a parking spot and remember to tell Richard, her son, where the car was parked. There always are so many crazy things like

that you have to overcome, but God was always with us
and He took care of me. There were so many nice people
along the way who helped me.

— *Mary Schoendienst*

One of those people was Stoneham, who had made arrangements with the airline to allow Mary and the girls to board the plane early, giving them more time to get settled. I was going to pick them up when they landed in Milwaukee, and I was real excited to see them again, even though we only had been separated for a few days. I got to the airport early and settled in at the gate, waiting for the plane.

The problem was the plane was late, and while I was waiting, it came in at a different gate, and I didn't hear it announced. I finally looked up at the monitor, and noticed what had happened.

What I didn't know at that time was that Mary was still sitting on the plane, refusing to get off because she didn't see me waiting for her. I guess she was so worked up about the trade and everything, she wanted some assurance in seeing me, and until she did, she wasn't going to budge.

The stewardess was calling someone and saying,
"There's somebody on this plane with three children and
she is not getting off." The pilot came back to talk to me,
and I told him I wasn't getting off until I saw my husband.
It was hard for me.

— *Mary Schoendienst*

It didn't take long for us to get adjusted to Milwaukee. I had been there only a couple of days when the manager, Fred Haney, said he wanted to make me the captain of the team. Haney had been the one who kept bugging GM John Quinn about making the trade to bring me to the Braves. When Haney told me his idea about naming me captain, I said, "Oh no, forget about that. I just got here, and you've got Hank Aaron, Del Crandall, Eddie Mathews, Johnny Logan, Joe Adcock, Frank Torre and other guys. No, I'm not going to be the captain. I'll do anything you want me to do and I'll play hard. That's about all I can do."

That team had been playing well before I got there and had a lot of established veterans. The last thing I wanted to do was come in there and disrupt the chemistry and mess up the attitudes of all the good ballplayers they had, and have them all mad at me.

That didn't turn out to be a problem. I joined the Braves in Philadelphia, and got a terrific reception.

> *I'll never forget it. Red came in to the clubhouse and put on the Braves' uniform and it made us all feel like Superman. We knew he was going to mean so much to our ballclub that wouldn't show up in the boxscore. He provided the leadership in the clubhouse and on the field. We knew that if there was a runner on second and no outs, Red wasn't going to strike out. He was going to get him to third base. He was never a rah-rah college kind of guy, but he definitely became the leader of that ballclub.*
>
> *— Hank Aaron*

Mary also had a quick indoctrination to the Milwaukee fans, and she was as well-received and accepted as I had been by the players on the team.

> *The town was so excited about having Red, they said that's all the team needed. They had a program at the time that featured the wives of the players. They called me immediately and asked me to go on, and I tried to get out of it by saying I had just gotten in town. They said, "Can't you make it on Saturday?" I said I would try, and I did go on the show.*
>
> *After the show, I had things to do. I had to go to the butcher shop and to get groceries. When I went in the store people recognized me because they had seen me on television. That was terrible. I didn't want to be recognized. Everybody in town was cheering for that team. It was incredible. It was an exciting time for us to be there.*
>
> *— Mary Schoendienst*

The people in Milwaukee had been so excited to get a team when the Braves had moved from Boston in 1953, and that excitement had not worn out. It was a friendly town, and it was always fun to play in front of good fans when you had a good ballclub.

It was kind of ironic that the Braves were playing the Cardinals when I got to Milwaukee, and the Cardinals were the team we were battling for the pennant during the stretch drive in September. It really wasn't that strange playing against the Cardinals, because one of the things I prided myself on was being ready to play when I got to the ballpark and playing hard, regardless of the opponent or the circumstances.

The strangest part was when I got to first base, and stood there next to Musial, my roommate for 10 years. We never talked. I very seldom talked on the ballfield. After the game was over we talked. As close as we had been, however, we never talked when we were on opposing teams. Not many guys talked to players on other teams back then. You really didn't even want the guys on the other team standing around watching while you were taking batting practice. It really was a more competitive game, almost like war. You had to find a way to win somehow; that was the only thing that mattered.

I always respected that style of play, and I never really thought anybody who took a hard slide into second base was trying to hurt me, only trying to break up a double play. The only exception was one time in Philadelphia, when we were getting beat and I took a throw at second base for a force out, the third out of the inning. I was on the outfield side of the base, away from the runner, but Puddinhead Jones kept running and hit me hard. We exchanged some words, and I really wanted him to get on first base again. He did, and I told the shortstop that if the ball went back to the pitcher, I was taking the throw. The batter hit a groundball to third, and I took the throw. He came in sliding, and I jumped up and came down with my spike just beneath his right ear. I cut him, but I pulled up. I could have really hurt him if I'd wanted to. He looked up at me and said, "Oh, I guess you mean what you say."

Obviously, playing for the pennant instead of on a second-division team is a more pressure-filled situation, but that never bothered me. I was much happier being in a winning, successful environment, and we had so many stars on the Braves that it was easy to spread the attention and notoriety around.

Haney at the time gave me a lot of credit for being a take-charge guy on the infield, and that made me feel good.

Frankly, he's been doing a better job than I anticipated. Since we gave up a lot to get him, we expected a lot. But he's really exceeded all of our expectations. His hitting and own personal play has been better for us than it was against us.

But his biggest value to the club is the way he has taken charge on the field. That was the big reason we wanted him in the first place. And when he first reported to us, I asked him to take over that role.

The boys listen to Schoendienst, where they and players on other clubs wouldn't listen to others, because he is a likeable, modest fellow. He's not a pop-off. By his very experience and personality, he commands respect.

— *Fred Haney*

I do think that when you are surrounded by players who are gung-ho and have a good positive attitude, it rubs off on the other guys. I learned a lot playing as a youngster around guys like Terry Moore and Enos Slaughter, and I saw the way they helped and offered encouragement to me and other young players, and when I got the chance to serve in that role with the Braves, I was more than happy to do it.

Sometimes I'll be having trouble at the plate, and I'll be a little down. But then Red starts talking to me. Now ordinarily I resent that from somebody else. But that guy just seems to have a certain way with him and before long I'll be back hitting that ball.

He's constantly yelling to Johnny (Logan) or Eddie Mathews at third or to me. Say it's late in the game and a fellow has a tendency to relax. Red'll be forever yelling to stay alive out there. In the dugout, after we have scored maybe four runs, he'll keep saying "more runs. Let's get more runs."

— Frank Torre

Being a leader on the field was just something that came naturally for me. I learned by watching the way Slaughter and Moore played and led by example and that was the kind of player I wanted to be. You didn't win pennants by just going through the motions, you had to play hard and you had to know what you were doing.

That style of play rubbed off on all of the Milwaukee guys, and it really was a talented team. We had Joe Adcock and Frank Torre on first, Johnny Logan at short, Eddie Mathews at third, Del Crandall catching and Aaron, Wes Covington and Bill Bruton in the outfield. On the pitching staff we had Warren Spahn, Lew Burdette and Bob Buhl, just to name a few.

Playing with Aaron and watching him perform on the field was a great thrill, just as it had been with Musial and Mays. To me, the best ballplayers I ever played with or against were Musial, Aaron and Mays. There were a lot of great players in the American League too like Williams, DiMaggio and Mantle, but I never got to see them every day like I did those three guys. You are not going to find better ballplayers than Musial and Aaron. Mays belongs in that group as well, because he also was a tremendously talented, natural player.

Aaron was like Musial in the sense that he would just come out and do his job without fanfare and didn't make something look hard when it was easy. He made everything look easy. People talk today about guys hitting 30 homers and stealing 30 bases. Aaron could have done that easily, and so could Mays, but teams didn't play that style of baseball then. Aaron had great judgment on the field, and always seemed to know when to take the extra base and when not to. The other thing I appreciated about Hank was that he laughed all the time. He really enjoyed playing and that showed in his actions on the field and in the clubhouse.

Some people were talking after Aaron and Mays had been in the league a few years that Mays might have the best shot of breaking Babe Ruth's home record. I spoke out in favor of Aaron, saying he also was the kind of guy who might be able to break it. People said he was a line-drive hitter, but he also hit 30 or more homers every year. He was just a steady ballplayer in all phases of the game.

The first time I saw Aaron play was in spring training when I was still with the Cardinals and he was just coming up with the Braves. Anybody could tell he was going to be something special. He just had that look about him in everything he did on the field— snapping his wrists when he was hitting, running and throwing, he was just a natural. He knew what he was doing.

I always appreciated the fact he was kind to me, and credited me with playing a key role in helping that club mature and find a way to win.

> *The guys who were playing everyday didn't have a lot of experience. Red had been through a pennant chase. He kept everybody glued together and doing what they had to do. The year before, 1956, we had lost the pennant by one game and we were on the verge of probably doing the same thing again before he joined the ballclub.*
>
> *He gave us what we needed to make that club the kind of club we became. He was just a tremendous ballplayer. He and I dressed side-by-side and I'll never forget how much he taught me about the game. He was a terrific leader.*
>
> *—Hank Aaron*

The talent on that team was amazing. Crandall was just 19 years old when he reached the majors with the Braves in 1949, and to come up at that age as a catcher you've got to be something special. The most unusual things about him was how much he knew at that age—both about the game in general and how to call a game. He was one of the best I ever played with.

Mathews was a raw player. He was tough. He played hard, and he played to win, out of the Enos Slaughter school of baseball. No matter what he had to do, he was going to win.

My partner in the middle of the infield, Logan, was a fun guy to be around. He knew how to play, but he always wanted to know more and learn what to do in different situations. He was always asking questions, and I'm sure he was that way before I got to Milwaukee. He was one of a group of players who liked to sit around and talk about the game, and that fit in with my personality and style as well. They would get on one another as well, in a good-natured manner, and that ensured that we had a good time playing, like the game is supposed to be.

It also was enjoyable to be on the field playing behind a guy like Spahn, one of the best pitchers in the history of the game. Playing behind him was easy, because you knew he was going to be around the plate. He worked fast and he threw strikes. It was the same way playing behind Burdette, because he had an idea of what he was doing on the mound. He kept the ball down, and you could almost feel that the ball was going to be hit to you.

I enjoyed all of the guys on that team, because they were serious when it was time to be serious about the game and ready to have fun off the field, especially when it came to playing some well-planned practical jokes or two. One of the guys' favorite targets was Donald Davidson, our traveling secretary.

Donald was a great guy. He suffered from a rare disease. He never grew after age 6, when he was 4 foot tall. He never let that interfere with his work and his appreciation of the game. He was one of the hardest working people that I was ever around in baseball, and everybody on the team really appreciated him and did anything we could to help him. He dished out as many jokes as people played on him, and that's what made it fun.

One Saturday afternoon after a game, we walked out of the ballpark and Donald's car was sitting in his parking space, which had about a two or three-foot concrete barrier behind it. Burdette and Buhl and a couple of other guys picked that car up, and set the back bumper on that barrier, leaving his rear wheels three or four inches off the ground. Donald came out, and didn't notice it, and started up his car, the wheels turned but he didn't go anywhere. He had a real strange look on his face. When we all came to the park the next morning, the car was still sitting there. He must have had to take a cab home, or spent the night at the ballpark.

Donald's response when he found out who had played the trick was to say, "The next room you get on the road isn't going to be very good. I'll put you in some kind of place." He was a dandy.

The guy on that team I hadn't been as familiar with playing against the Braves was Logan, the shortstop. He was a great player, and I don't think he ever received the recognition he should have received. Torre was a great hitter, and it was a shame he couldn't run better or he would have hit for a lot higher average. His average every year would have been well over .300 if he could have just run a little.

That team had a lot of confidence in its ability. They had won 92 games the previous year, losing the pennant to the Dodgers by only one game, and you could see the desire in their eyes from the minute I joined the ballclub. We ended up winning 95 games, and beat the second-place Cardinals by eight games to win the pennant and move on to the World Series, where the Yankees—and my old teammate, Slaughter—were waiting.

The Series opened in New York with a classic pitchers duel, Spahn against Whitey Ford. Ford prevailed, but we came back the next day behind Burdette to even the Series at a game each as we moved home to Milwaukee.

The Yankees dampened the Milwaukee fans' spirits with a 12-3 romp, but we had Spahn ready for Game Four and he carried a 4-1 lead into the ninth, only to give up two two-out singles and a homer to Elston Howard that tied the game and sent it into extra innings. The Yankees scored again in the top of the 10th, but Logan's RBI double tied the game and Mathews delivered a two-run blast to win the game for Spahn.

Burdette took matters into his own hands in Game Five, pitching a 1-0 shutout to beat Ford. The Yankees came back to win Game Six in New York, 3-2 on a homer by Hank Bauer to force the deciding seventh game.

Burdette came back to pitch on only two days rest and scattered four hits over eight innings as we built a 5-0 lead. We got two outs in the bottom of the ninth, and were preparing to celebrate when the Yankees loaded the bases. Bill Skowron was the hitter, and he hit a sharp grounder just inside third base. Mathews was able to smother it and step on third for the game's final out to let the partying begin.

Even though we won, I really didn't feel much like partying. A pulled groin muscle, suffered in the fifth game when I tried to field a ball hit over second base by Slaughter, had forced me to sit out the last two games of the series. I also was tired, so much so that I didn't even take Mary to see "The Music Man" on Broadway while we were in New York.

> *Everybody went except Red and me. I asked Red why he didn't get tickets, and he said, "I've got news for you. We're going to win it again next year and I'll take you then." We did win, and we went to the show. I made him stick to his promise. He played the Series, but I knew he was very sick then. He hung in there and did what he had to do.*
>
> *— Mary Schoendienst*

I was happy for Haney, because he was a good guy and a good manager. He was the kind of guy who ran a disciplined club, and he made certain everybody was fundamentally sound and knew what they were supposed to do in every situation. He had a veteran ballclub, and he had a good relationship with the players. They respected the fact he was the manager, and that he knew what he was doing, and was making the moves he thought would give the team its best chance of winning.

Fred was the kind of manager who was a friend of the players, but he also knew he was the manager and drew the line at becoming real buddy-buddy with them. That's one of the hardest things a manager has to do, be able to have that good positive friendship with his players but also be able to become the boss when the situation calls for it. That's the same for managers today as it was when I played and also when I managed.

The vote for the National League's Most Valuable Player was close, and I was glad I wasn't asked to cast a ballot. Aaron ended up winning, beating out Musial by nine points, 239 to 230. In third place, with 221 points, was me. I was thankful for that support from the baseball writers and was glad to be in the company of two of the greatest players in the game's history.

The fans in St. Louis were as nice to me as the writers. Even though the Braves had beaten the Cardinals for the pennant, I still found people to be as pleasant to me when I came back to St. Louis for the winter as they had been when I was playing for the Cardinals. I spent time helping the Lions Club sell Christmas trees, and people were constantly coming up to me and congratulating me and wishing me and the Braves well in the coming season.

I was excited about our chances of repeating in 1958, because the team was returning virtually intact. I got off to a quick start and was hitting .313 on May 20, but then I ran into more health problems, which had started in spring training and never got better all year.

A virus attack kept me out of the lineup for four days. After playing three games, I was sidelined again by what doctors first thought was a pulled chest muscle but turned out to be pleurisy. I had injured myself making a bad slide and was afraid at first I either had pulled some ligaments or cracked some ribs. The injury kept me out of the lineup for more than two weeks, and even after I returned to the lineup, I struggled for a month. I felt I was just getting my timing and strength back when I went down again, this time suffering a broken finger when I was hit on the left hand while trying to bunt.

We were lucky none of the players or others traveling with the club were hurt when a plane we were taking home from the West Coast had a close call one night. It seemed like when you went over Pueblo, Colorado, you always hit an air pocket. That's what we did on that night, and some of the guys were playing cards and pinochle in the back of the plane, including little Donald Davidson. I was in my seat sitting down, and we hit that air pocket.

It looked like everybody who wasn't wearing their seat belts just flew up out of their seats. Little Donald was in mid-air. It looked like the guys were just hanging halfway between the ceiling and the floor. The plane shook like mad. It felt like it was going to break in half. I don't know why it didn't, it shook that hard.

Nobody got hurt. Burdette grabbed ahold of Donald, which was easy for him since he was such a big guy. Everybody was pretty shook up, however. I don't know how that plane stuck together.

I ended up playing only 106 games in 1958, and my average and general health kept sliding. I even made two errors in one game, and Haney did the right thing when he sent up a pinch-hitter for me in some situations. It hurt, but I knew I wasn't helping the team, and people who had seen me play for a long time noticed the difference. They told me I was "choking" the bat higher than normal, which left me little chance of getting a hit. If we had not been fighting for the pennant, some of the guys might have noticed earlier that something was wrong, but they were too concerned with whether the team was winning or losing to try to figure out what was wrong with me.

I knew something was wrong, however, but I also was determined to get through the World Series before I saw a doctor. I had an idea what he was going to tell me, and I didn't want to hear it.

Playing in the World Series must have pumped me up a little bit, because I had nine hits, tying Aaron for the most on our club, and scored five runs as we jumped to a 3-1 lead over the Yankees. We couldn't get a key hit when we needed it in any of the last three games, however. We lost the sixth game 4-3 in 10 innings to set up game seven for the second consecutive year. We were tied 2-2 going into the eighth inning, but the Yankees came up with four runs, three coming on a homer from Skowron, and they won the game and the Series.

I had put off going to the doctor almost as long as possible. Mary was pregnant with our fourth child, who turned out to be our only boy, Kevin, and I was determined to wait until the baby was born and Mary was OK before finding out what was wrong with me. Kevin was born November 3, and five days later I was in the hospital. I really was afraid it was going to be something serious.

Chapter 7

FIGHTING A DISEASE

My oldest brother, Andy, and his wife came to Milwaukee for a visit just before the 1958 season ended. It was a Saturday, and Andy said that when he arrived at the house, I was just lying there. They were staying at a motel anyway, but he said he just looked at me and decided to leave me alone.

He could tell I was sick. It wasn't my nature to just lay around and rest all day. I like to be active, up and going. When you don't feel well, however, it's hard to force your body into action. Since I was still playing, and we were in a pennant race, I suppose subconsciously I was trying to save all of my strength for the games. Every day it felt like we had played three doubleheaders. That's how drained I was when the day was over.

Andy told the story of how the day after he saw me looking so sickly, he went to the game at County Stadium and watched me go four-for-four. There weren't many days like that, however.

It was about the same time that a friend, a writer from St. Louis, came up to me before a game and asked what was wrong. He hadn't seen me for a while, and he could tell I didn't look well. I tried to pass it off that I was just suffering from a bad cold, but in my own mind, I was scared.

During the World Series when I was in the field, I couldn't move. When I walked up to bat, I could hardly swing the bat. I saw the ball well and everything, but I couldn't react to it. There was no question I was sick. Sitting in front of my locker one day, I looked over to Frank Torre and said, "I feel terrible and I'm just not old enough to feel this bad."

After the series ended and we came back to St. Louis, the decision couldn't be postponed any longer. As soon as Mary went to the hospital to give birth to Kevin, the appointment for me to see the doctor was scheduled.

Dr. Sam Merenda took some X-rays and noticed something that he thought needed to be examined further. He sent me to see Dr. William Werner at St. John's Hospital, who took more X-rays and ran more tests. When those results came back, he knew what the problem was.

He walked into the room where I was waiting for the results, and told me, "Red, I've got great news for you. You've got tuberculosis."

After letting that news sink into my brain for a couple of seconds, the incongruity of his statement got to me. "Doc, how do you figure that's good?" I asked.

The doctor said, "We know what it is. And we know where it is. Now we go after it."

That logic made sense to me, and the other decision I made in that room was that I was going to fight this disease as hard as I had played any game in my life. I had too much to live for—a great wife, four happy and healthy kids, the desire to return and play baseball again—to surrender without waging all-out war.

To do that, I pledged that day to do whatever the doctor said, to become a model patient and listen to him as closely as I ever listened to any manager and coach.

Transferred to Mount Saint Rose sanitorium, I knew I was facing months of lying in bed doing practically nothing. They had developed some great medicine, but the biggest cure was rest, giving the body time to heal. That gave me a lot of time to think and reflect, and what I determined was that I was lucky.

Doctors had been taking X-rays of my chest for years, and they determined I probably had been carrying the TB germ for a long time. In the 1940s, doctors told me the shadow they saw on my lung apparently was from an old ailment that was no longer a problem.

Having the extra time to think, it was clear to me that I had been suffering from the illness for a long time, but it had never reached the point where I couldn't perform and play. It had to be the explanation why I always got tired the second half of the season, after July, when I just seemed to lose all my energy. I thought about how when I was out of the lineup for a few days because of an injury, I always seemed to come back with a little extra zip and performed better. That had to be the reason.

I also realized I was lucky doctors had caught the problem when they did, when it was still treatable. If it had gone undetected for much longer, it might have been too advanced for the medicine and rest to do any good.

What wasn't spoken at the time was that I was afraid I had cancer. If anything, I felt good that I didn't have cancer. Tuberculosis was bad enough, and it was worse in those days than it is now, but it still was better than cancer. There was basically nothing they could do for you if you had cancer back then, except try to make you comfortable for whatever time you had left. When the doctor told me I had TB, I had no doubt that I was going to make a complete recovery, and do it more quickly than some people expected.

When the announcement was made public, a lot of people thought my career was over. I was 35, and had not played well in 1958. I knew the reason for that poor season, however, was my illness. If anything, that only increased my desire to come back and play and play well, so I wouldn't end my career with that disappointing performance.

It was hard just lying in bed, sleeping and watching television, when I was used to going out everyday in the winter to hunt or fish. It was what I had to do to get better, however, and that was my goal so it was what I did. I told the doctors there were two things I would like to do: When I got up in the morning, I wanted to shave, brush my teeth myself and take a shower. I wanted to do the same thing in the evening. I had a private room, and the bathroom and shower was about 10 to 20 feet away from my bed, and they said that was fine. More than anything else what they wanted to do was relax me, and they thought it would be good for me.

What I couldn't do was hold and talk with my kids. Nobody under 16 was allowed in the hospital room—room 327, a nice corner room with a big window—and that was tough. It was hard to look at my three girls and new son Kevin out that window and not be able to take them in my arms and wrap them up with a big hug and kiss.

One of the people who really helped me when I was in the hospital was Babe Linneman, Joe's wife. I don't remember all of this happening, but Mary and Babe told me later that she was the only one I really trusted part of the time because she was a registered nurse. She was working, and it was hard for her to get to Mount Saint Rose, but I said, "Tell Babe to get down here. I want her to come." It was about 15 miles from where she was working, and she had to take a streetcar and then transfer to a bus. It took about an hour and a half to get there. She came three nights in a row, and I really appreciated it.

Babe and Joe always did so much for our family, especially during those months I was in the hospital. Babe would come over and help Mary with the kids, and sometimes the kids would go to their house. Babe would have them make cupcakes or something, and they always had a great time. Later, when I was out of the hospital, the kids still wanted to go over there and hang out with Babe and Joe.

Red and Mary would have a big night out, so we were the babysitters. I don't think he ever paid me for that either.
— Joe Linneman

It was amazing to me that the news of my illness received the attention it did. People whom I had never met and never had any contact with in my life were writing me letters of support and encouragement. It really meant a lot to me that so many people took the time to write and offer their good wishes. I was sorry I couldn't respond to each letter personally.

One letter came in and went unnoticed for a few days until my father-in-law happened upon it in the box with all of the other letters. The small printing in the top left hand corner, the return address, caught his attention: The White House.

He opened it, and saw the signature at the end of the letter—Dwight D. Eisenhower—and showed it to Mary. She knew I hadn't seen it or I would have said something about it.

The letter read:

> *"I have just heard the news concerning your illness. I am confident that before long you will again take your place on the playing field as one of the great ballplayers of our time.*
>
> *"Anyone with the competitive spirit that you have so often demonstrated can lick this thing. And you are not alone in your fight. Baseball fans throughout the country are pulling for you and wishing you a speedy and complete recovery. My own hopes and prayers will be with you.*
>
> *"With best wishes, sincerely, Dwight D. Eisenhower."*

While I was in the hospital, I received more than 10,000 pieces of mail, mostly cards and letters. Four big cardboard boxes were stuffed with letters.

The letters came from U.S. soldiers in Germany, an entire classroom from Canada, classmates from Colleen's school in Milwaukee, a lot of my ex-teammates in St. Louis and New York and current teammates with the Braves, almost every player on the Yankees, former Army mates, every member of the Green Bay Packers football team, restaurateur Toots Shor and others who were just fans of mine or fans of baseball in general. Every letter meant a lot to me.

More letters and cards poured in before Christmas, which I spent in that hospital room. The nuns helped decorate the room, including putting up two Christmas trees. One, the artificially frosted kind, was a gift from the Lions Club in recognition of all those years

I had helped sell trees at their lot. There was a red stocking, with "Al Schoendienst" printed in white on top, hanging from the foot of my bed. The nuns had filled it with an apple, an orange, cookies and a candy stick.

One classroom of kids sent me a giant card, and another sent me a long roll with a message telling me to hurry up and get well. It was covered with valentines they made in class.

A lot of players, including Robin Roberts and Carl Erskine, called to visit on the telephone. As soon as I was allowed to have visitors, Stan Musial came by regularly and a lot of other guys also visited, including Braves' teammates Eddie Mathews and Gene Conley. Conley was trying a basketball comeback and stopped by when he was in town with the Boston Celtics.

Manager Fred Haney came to town to check up on me, as did the Braves' Harry Hansbrink and Del Rice. I also received a combined visit one day from Yogi Berra and Joe Garagiola.

Yogi was being honored at a dinner, and Joe wanted me to make a tape with him that they could play at the dinner. I had been watching a football game between the Colts and Giants when they entered the room, and the set was still on. Yogi sat down and started rooting for the Giants.

Kidding him, I said "I guess I'll just have to root for the Colts then." Yogi then suggested we put a little wager on the outcome. They left before the game was over, and I had to remind Yogi later about what he owed me. It was strange how he seemed to forget about the bet.

Having visitors like that and telephone calls broke up the monotony of the day, where every day was exactly the same as the one before. If I hadn't been so committed to following the doctor's orders exactly, I might have become more restless. I trusted their advice, however, and I knew that the more I rested and let the medicine work, the quicker I would recover and be allowed to go home.

One thing I was able to do was watch television, which was a lifesaver. I watched a lot of sports, and to save the energy required to get out of bed to turn it off and on, I was able to figure out how to pull the little knob out and push it back in with my toes. The nuns were entertained by that—I don't know if anyone had ever been that creative before.

The nuns who took care of me were wonderful, caring women. Mary and I had become friends with one, Sister Mary Jeanne, who had written me a fan letter years before. She prepared all of my meals, and made certain I had good food and plenty of it. There were no complaints about the hospital food she prepared. I gained so much weight in the hospital I had to stop eating desserts. She is a great lady, and we still stay in contact with her.

When I got stronger and was feeling better, Dr. Werner told me there was another way to speed my recovery—surgery, to remove the part of my lung that was infected. My reaction was, "Let's do it."

The morning of the surgery, Mary was in the elevator at the hospital when Dr. Joseph Lucido arrived, about 6:30 a.m. Mary had never met him, but he introduced himself and she looked at him and noticed that he had cut himself with a razor when he was shaving. He told Mary, "I'm going to be the one doing the operation."

Imagine what I was thinking. I said to Dr. Werner, "Are you sure that man was the best you could find?" He said, "Mary, he's from St. Louis University and he's the best." I said, "Well do you know he cut himself shaving this morning? Do you think he was a little nervous?" I was really concerned. Dr. Werner looked at me and told me not to worry.

— Mary Schoendienst

Dr. Lucido had told me the day before that he was going to perform the surgery so that he wouldn't have to cut any muscles. He was a big baseball fan, and he told me I actually would be better than I was before when he was finished, and he turned out to be right. He took out a rib and clipped out a little segment of my lung, the only part that was affected by the TB. The doctors said the TB was located in a section of the lung that was kind of like a spare tire on an automobile. They took a small piece out of it, and you couldn't even see it on the X-ray. I wasn't worried. I had a lot of confidence in

Dr. Lucido. He had told me, "I'll take my time doing it and you will play again." I knew everything was going to work out.

So did the Braves. Before the surgery, some special visitors showed up in my hospital room. Executive Vice President Birdie Tebbetts stopped by on his way home after watching Milwaukee prospects playing winter ball in the Caribbean, and John Quinn, the team GM, and Donald Davidson came down from Milwaukee.

Quinn and Tebbetts told me they wanted to negotiate my contract for 1959 on a normal basis, as if I had not gotten sick. Even though their proposal called for a small pay cut, I wasn't in a very favorable bargaining position. After all, my average had slumped to .262 the year before, cause normally—in those days—for a cut in salary. Considering I wasn't certain when, or if, I would be playing in 1959 I considered the offer very generous and took the deal without argument.

The Braves' owner, Lou Perini, knew I might not play a game in 1959 but he still wanted me to have that salary and I certainly appreciated it. Had the team not been willing to do that I am certain it would have added a lot of mental stress to wonder how I would take care of my family, and giving me that contract allowed me to concentrate entirely on getting well and playing again.

Signing me was Quinn's last act as general manager of the Braves. I didn't know it, but he already had agreed to become the GM of the Phillies—it was going to be announced the next day—but wanted to get me back under contract before he left. I always appreciated that gesture on his part.

I really didn't know how good he was until I had a chance to see him play every day for the Braves. He wasn't a holler guy, but he was a leader just the same. Even pitchers like Spahn and Burdette listened when Red came trotting in to the mound.

— John Quinn

Quinn always was very good to me, and that was one of the reasons why, when I was healthier, I dropped him a note to thank him for all the kindness he had shown me over the years.

I wrote, "I'm sorry you left the Braves, but you will probably like the Phillies, too. Just don't get too good for us. I wish you all the best of luck within those limits. Thanks for all the nice things you did for me, and I'll be seeing you one of these days."

As I got stronger and began feeling better, I wondered what kind of player I would have been had I had more stamina, had I not gotten so tired and run-down in the second half of every season. Six months after the operation, I felt better at age 36 than I had when I was in my 20s. I had played sick for so long I didn't know what it was like to be healthy when I was playing.

One of my cousins was in a mood to celebrate after the surgery, and he came to the hospital one day with a big bucket with a bottle of champagne in it. The nuns had other ideas, and even I didn't think mixing that alcohol with all that medicine was probably a very good idea.

Dr. Lucido was correct about my recovery. One of the side effects of the surgery was throughout my career I always had been plagued by a sore arm. Afterward, I never had a sore arm. The rib grew back. Before the TB was found I had suffered from pneumonia, the whooping cough and I always seemed to have a cold. Ever since the operation, I seldom even get a bad cold anymore.

I also was ready to get out of that hospital, and when the day came that the doctors finally told me I could go home, it gave me a feeling of great relief.

I had entered Mount Saint Rose on November 12, undergone the surgery on February 19, and walked out of the hospital on March 24, a much healthier and happier man. I had gained 10 pounds, something most people don't do on hospital food.

One worry they had, however, was that I would try to overdo things simply because I was out of their care and constant watch. I still wasn't ready to play baseball, I still had to rest a great deal, but I could do what I wanted to do most, spend time with Mary and the kids, finally, for the first time, picking up and hugging my by-then four-month-old son, Kevin.

Mary made certain I took things easy, but she also kept me busy so I wouldn't be thinking too much about trying to come back and play before I was physically ready. Being out of the hospital was great, but I was still a long way from being totally cured. Try having to take 24 pills a day and see how you like it.

There finally was time to catch up on all of the letters I had received, and it still amazes me how many people whom I had never meant took the time to write and send me their wishes. I learned there are a lot of wonderful people in the world. That was one lesson I remembered last year when it was reported that young Mets' pitcher Jason Isringhausen had been diagnosed with TB. I wrote him a letter and told him what I had gone through and how I knew he would be OK if he just listened to his doctors and did what they told him.

Mary, the kids and I did a lot of fun things while I was home. We went fishing, horseback riding and water skiing. We went on picnics, and we went to a family reunion. All my brothers and sister and their kids were there. We went to the Lake of the Ozarks and stayed for several weeks, where I mostly laid in the sun, swam a little and rested. Mary kind of enjoyed having me home in the summer for the first time and not playing baseball. There was something missing, however, and that was getting me back on the field again.

I knew I had been lucky, and I wanted to show how grateful I was and one way to do that was by doing public relations work for the National Tuberculosis Association. I also knew I could perform a valuable function by getting back on the field playing, showing that a person can come back from TB and return to what they were doing and live a normal life.

In July, I started exercising. I did bending exercises to get my legs in shape and arm exercises to strengthen my shoulders. I started playing catch with some of the kids in the neighborhood and also my father-in-law. The doctors told me the only thing they didn't want me doing was running. They even let me go out and play golf.

My brother Joe and I started going around to different parks in St. Louis where he had more room and didn't attract too much attention. We played pepper, and I started to get my eyes used to focusing on a baseball and trying to hit it again.

The Braves came to St. Louis for a series against the Cardinals, and I went to Busch Stadium to meet the guys and also to get in some live swings for the first time since the World Series. It was early in the morning, and it gave me a warm glow to walk out on the field and stand at home plate, ready to hit against Bob Giggie, a hard-throwing rookie. I took three turns in the cage, about 75 swings in all, batting lefthanded and hit some line drives around the park. I even slammed two pitches against the pavilion screen in right field. It felt good, great even, but I had to warn myself that one morning of batting practice didn't mean I was ready to play again against pitchers who were trying to exploit my weaknesses and get me out.

I also went out to my second base position and fielded some easy grounders, shagged some fly balls and even jogged a little. I knew Fred Haney and the guys were paying close attention to me, wondering how well I was doing, and it was reassuring to me and them to know my comeback was coming along nicely. The best feeling for me was that I didn't get tired, which told me I already was better than I had been when I was playing the year before.

Some of the guys on the team got a little lift by seeing me work out as well, and I was glad I had helped the team in that way.

An indication of what his presence meant to the ballclub was that there was nobody who could take his place. He didn't hit 40 homers or have a .330 average, but he did a lot of things to help our club in the locker room and on the field. We didn't get that help when Red wasn't there.

— Hank Aaron

The Braves left town and went on with their season, and I stayed home in St. Louis. The Cardinals were kind enough to say I could continue to work out at the ballpark, which I did every day, going early to get some batting practice in before the Cardinals and their opponents needed to take the field to get ready for that day's game.

If the doctors had had their way, I probably would not have tried to play until the following spring training, but it really was important for me to get back into the lineup playing in September, so I didn't miss a complete season. I didn't want to do anything foolish after having been so careful and precise with every other phase of my treatment and recovery, but this was one area where I felt I knew more than the doctors. Dr. Werner said he knew I would be able to pinch-hit OK, but he didn't know about playing in the field. He finally said it was up to me, and as long as I and the Braves were willing to be cautious and not overdo things, he would give his OK.

Part of the reason I was in such a hurry to get back was I was hoping I could contribute something down the stretch that would help the team win its third pennant in a row. Second base had been a problem spot for the team all year. The young player who was supposed to take my place, Mel Roach, had suffered a severe knee injury which had knocked him out of action. Haney had been forced to juggle seven players at the position—Roach, Chuck Cottier, Casey Wise, Johnny O'Brien, Joe Morgan, Felix Mantilla and Bobby Avila. We were in third place, behind Los Angeles and San Francisco, and Haney really was hoping my return would prove a spark to the team, not only because of what I could do on the field but just being around the team and in the locker room and dugout providing an emotional lift.

Before I had gotten sick, I often said I intended to play until I was 40 and getting back on the field reinforced that goal in my mind. I loved playing, and probably only when I got back on the field did I fully realize and appreciate how much I had missed it when I was away.

Following the doctor's orders, undergoing the surgery, lying in bed for all those months, taking all those pills—everything involved in my comeback—flashed through my mind when I was sitting on the bench during a game against the Phillies and Haney called for me to grab a bat and pinch-hit for pitcher Juan Pizarro.

We were losing, 7-4, in the seventh inning, but the ovation I received from the 18,000 fans at County Stadium could not have been greater if the park was filled. The cheers sent goosebumps down my back, and I stepped out of the box to get a couple of extra moments to try to compose myself.

I'd like to say the comeback was topped with a dramatic homer, but the record books will show that I grounded back to pitcher Robin Roberts, who threw me out at first.

The fans cheered again, and the media raved about how heroic a comeback it was. That part of the story bothered me because quite honestly, I wanted people to forget the fact I had recovered from TB and just treat me like a normal person. The doctors did all of the work, I just laid there and did what I was told. I honestly didn't consider it that dramatic or major of a story, yet every reporter wanted to talk to me about it and tried to make the story bigger than it was. It really wasn't that tough.

I looked at it as if I was an automobile that got out of whack and had to be fixed. It needed new parts to run as well as it had before. In my case, they took out a part, and then I was as good as new.

Another aspect of my return that overwhelmed me was the next round of telegrams and letters I received. One letter came from Vice President Richard Nixon, and a telegram came from Gussie Busch.

"It was good news to hear that you have returned to the Braves' batting order. We joined in the ovation given you by your fans, in spirit, if not in fact. I want to congratulate you on a magnificent show of courage and determination. My sincerest congratulations, too, on your appointment as National Honorary Chairman of the 1959 Christmas Seal campaign of the Tuberculosis and Health Society, which I understand is to be announced Thursday. As always, our best wishes will be with you for all future success."

— August A. Busch Jr.

I played in five games in September, getting three at-bats but failing to get a hit. Just getting that limited work, however, told me what I needed to do to be ready for the 1960 season.

Even though I was wearing the uniform and was back with the team, it still didn't feel like I belonged there because I had missed so much of the season. We did catch the Dodgers, tying them for the pennant and forcing a best-of-three playoff series. I didn't play, and we lost the first two games, going down 6-5 in 12 innings in the final game. The Dodgers went on to the World Series and our two-year reign as league champions was over.

I also had a trip planned to Washington and New York in my honorary post as chairman of the Christmas Seal campaign. I've been fortunate to meet a lot of Presidents playing in the World Series and All-Star games, but a trip to the White House still was a special honor, and that's where Mary and I and the two older girls got to go in November. Unfortunately, President Eisenhower was busy that day, but we spent time with his wife, Mamie, and she was very nice to us.

She was very nice to the girls. Aunt Babe had given Colleen a bracelet for communion, and Mrs. Eisenhower liked it very much and wanted to get one for her granddaughter. Mrs. Eisenhower was talking to us and the secretary said, "Now we have to move on." Mrs. Eisenhower said, "Now just a moment, I would like to speak to these people." We had a little extra time with her. She was very nice to the girls.

I think they were afraid the children were going to do something to the room we were in. We were in the room where all the different presidents' china is displayed. The girls behaved themselves. Red jokes that they didn't sail any of the plates.

— Mary Schoendienst

On the same trip we went to New York, where we saw Eddie Fisher perform and he introduced me to the crowd as the national honorary chairman of the Christmas Seals. It was a fun night.

In New York, I did a film for the Tuberculosis Association with Dr. Dubose, one of the TB experts, and Charles Collingwood, the CBS newsman. Collingwood really impressed me. He was there about a half-hour before we were to begin filming, reading about three inches worth of newspapers. Somebody handed him his script of what he was supposed to say in the film, and he flipped through it so fast it was unbelievable. Everything that was asked of him, he knew what to say and what he was talking about. He just went through it and said, "Let's go" and he did it. That always stuck with me anytime I heard him later on the news.

The National Tuberculosis Association had a dinner in St. Louis in January 1960, and I received more telegrams of congratulations than I could count. What impressed me the most was some of the people who took the time to write, including politicians, entertainers, baseball people, the media and even Cardinal Spellman. Other telegrams came from the likes of Harry Truman, Ford Frick, Joe Cronin, Jackie Robinson, Toots Shor and Howard Cosell. It was nice to consider all of those people my friends.

My health had improved, and I really was looking forward to proving to everybody that I was well. It wasn't long before I was counting the days to spring training.

The only career goal I ever had in my life came true, to be a major league baseball player.

It didn't take long before I was feeling pressure in the major leagues. Johnny Pesky was one of the runners who bore down on me during the 1946 World Series.

My wedding day with Mary was one of the best days of my life.

The young couple
in the living room
of our first home
on Potomac Street
in 1948.

I know what it's like to be on the receiving end of a runner trying to break up a double play, and I wanted to make certain Jackie Robinson of the Dodgers knew I could dish it out too.

I had a lot of fun forming a double-play tandem with one of the best shortstops of all-time, Marty Marion.

Jumping is a good skill for a second baseman trying to avoid a runner. I didn't know I could jump that high unless I had too.

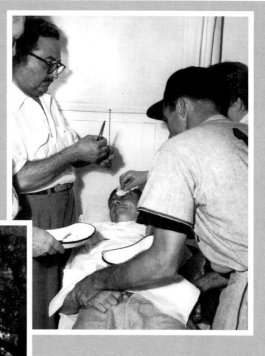

Dr. Anthony Palermo is preparing to stitch up my forehead after I was cut on a wild throw by Alvin Dark during a game against the Giants at the Polo Grounds in 1953.

I was a better hitter than I was a putter, thank goodness.

Part of a pretty good crowd, from left to right, Joe Garagiola, wrestler Lou Theiz, promoter Berstein, boxer Joe Louis, Stan Musial, Yogi Berra and me.

Those old flannel uniforms weighed a ton when you started to sweat, and check out how baggy the pants were. No wonder it was so hard to steal a base.

Mary and daughters Cathleen and Colleen were on hand for Germantown night, but the girls didn't like it when the dog got sick and threw up on them.

I tried wearing glasses, but they didn't help and the experiment quickly was abandoned.

My future team-
mate, Hank Aaron,
tries to break up a
double play.

Baseball isn't exactly ballet,
but sometimes you will do
anything to get out of the
way of a sliding runner, in
this case Gil Hodges of the
Dodgers.

Manager Bill Rigney welcomed
me to my new team, after my
pinch-hit homer in my New
York debut.

Mary and I welcomed
daughter Eileen soon after I
was traded to the Giants.

Check out the wheels. I'm standing with Wally Rank, an auto dealer
in Milwaukee who was a friend of many players.

After months in the
hospital, I finally felt up
to gripping a bat again.

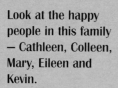

Daughters Colleen,
Cathleen and Eileen help
me look at some of the
mail that collected while I
was in the hospital.

Look at the happy
people in this family
— Cathleen, Colleen,
Mary, Eileen and
Kevin.

Manager Fred
Haney was ready
for me to rejoin the
Braves as soon as I
was ready.

Cathleen and Eileen
helped me get ready
to return to the
majors with some
backyard practice.

My first Christmas
back home after
recovering from
TB, in 1959, was
a happy occasion
for the
Schoendienst
family.

The people in
Germantown
always were
great to me, and
I appreciated all
of the support
they gave me.

One of the best players and
friends ever, Stan the Man.

First Lady Mamie
Eisenhower gave us a
presidential welcome
when Colleen,
Cathleen, Mary and I
visited the White House
in 1959 to publicize
the national Christmas
Seals campaign.

Dog Trainer Cotton Persell (left) and I taught Stan Musial (middle) all about hunting. He was a quick learner.

Flipping a ball around the house with the kids.

Johnny Keane and I were no doubt impressing this lady with our baseball knowledge.

Kevin and I check
out another sport in
the driveway.

Surrounded by coaches Joe
Becker, Bo Milliken, Dick Sisler
and Joe Schultz in 1966.

Part of a manager's job is facing
all those microphones.

It seemed like
the kids grew
up in a hurry.

Ready for the 1967
World Series and
my managerial
opponent, Dick
Williams of the Red
Sox.

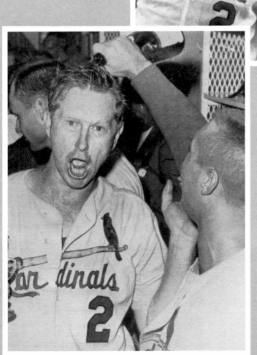

Winning the World Series is a
great feeling, even if champagne
does sting when it gets in your
eyes.

President Nixon was giving me some pointers about what to do in the 1968 World Series, but Tigers' manager Mayo Smith is listening in.

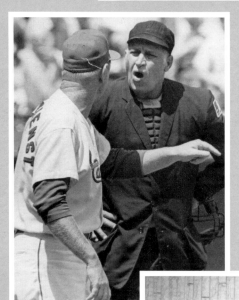

I got along with almost all of the umpires, but Kenny Burkhart and I didn't see eye-to-eye on this day.

Surrounded by some of the best in the game at a New York dinner. From left to right, me, Yogi Berra, Billy Martin, Willie Mays and Ralph Houk.

Sometimes you just have to sit down and put your feet up.

Two of the best bosses a guy could have, Gussie Busch and Whitey Herzog.

A longtime friend, Amadee Wohlschlager, always knows how to smile for the camera.

I've had a great ride through my baseball career, and I thank everybody who has shared the trip with me.

Chapter 8

ENDING ONE CAREER, STARTING ANOTHER

ny time a team changes managers, a player never knows exactly what the news is going to mean for him. When the Braves replaced Fred Haney before the 1960 season with Charley Dressen, it was bad news for me.

Haney and I had become close, developing a very good relationship, and he was somebody I believed I could confide in, who understood me and what I could do for a ballclub, and had the knowledge necessary to put his players in the situation where they had the best chance of succeeding and then left them alone to play and perform to the best of their abilities. He moved into the banking business in southern California, then went to work for NBC as a commentator on the games of the week. It wasn't long before he was back in the business on a full-time basis, taking the job as general manager of the expansion Angels.

For some reason, Dressen and I didn't develop that kind of relationship. He was the only difficult manager I ever played for. He would always say things like, "Hold them until the seventh and I'll figure out a way to win." He had kind of written me off because of the TB, and didn't think I could play anymore, even though I had a great spring training and deserved the starting job.

Part of the reason for my hot start was a diligent off-season workout program. A lot of players who lived in St. Louis in the winter, including Musial, Del Rice, Ken Boyer, Don Blasingame, Norm Siebern, Roy Sievers and Hal Smith, got together with Dr. Walter Eberhardt five times a week for a month. He directed us through a regiment of exercises and baseball drills, which especially helped me with my reflexes and got all of us in great shape when we reported to Florida.

There are a lot of good things about playing baseball for a living, but two of the best are having the chance to play and workout with guys like that and the second is going to Florida for spring training.

All those trips to St. Petersburg when I was with the Cardinals spoiled me, but the Braves' camp wasn't too far away, south of St. Petersburg in Bradenton. We played in old McKechnie Field, which is nothing like the new park there today—except that it's on the same site, but there are very few similarities between the spring training parks of today and the ones I played in.

The biggest difference was that we didn't have the complexes that the teams have today. We had one field, and that's where we had to do all our work. We spent a lot of time talking about the game, what we were going to do and how we were going to do it, and maybe that's something teams have gotten away from a little bit. Players of any generation don't really like to talk—they just want to go out and play.

No matter what situation you are in or what kind of facilities you have, a player has to make himself a better player no matter what the conditions are. It's a fun argument about how players of my or an earlier generation would do if they were playing today, but I don't think it's really a fair argument. If you talk about taking a guy and going back to when he was 21 or 22 years old, that would be one thing. If you could do that, the older players would be better because they could get used to the differences the players enjoy today. Nobody had anything then like they do today, so nobody knew what they were missing.

Reporting to Florida, I knew I was in good shape and playing even a little the previous September had told me I was completely recovered and ready for the full season. Dressen, however, had his doubts and that's why he was counting on Chuck Cottier to be his second baseman.

"I didn't count on Red," Dressen admitted in an interview at the time. "I wasn't sure he'd play at all, let alone every day. But he went down to camp and started hitting everybody. To watch him play, you would never know he ever had anything wrong with him."

I got off to a quick start as well, playing every day for the first two weeks and enjoying a nine-game hitting streak. I thought I had quieted the skeptics, but by the middle of July, Cottier had been called up from the minors and I was spending most of the time on the bench. Stories again were appearing in the newspapers that I was through and should consider retiring.

Mary went to Philadelphia to accept an award for me, and the headline in the newspaper there read, "Schoendienst's Comeback Fails." That hurt, because I knew I wasn't getting a fair chance to show what I could do.

Players always are a pretty good judge of themselves. You measure yourself against other players, and you know when you are doing well and when you are struggling. Even though I had worked hard to come back and wanted to fulfill my goal of playing until age 40, I wasn't going to embarrass myself or my team and continue to play if I wasn't physically able to do it.

Alvin Dark was a teammate then, and he was always on me to go into Dressen's office and talk to him about what was going on. I said, "I can't go talk to him," and I didn't. I never interfered with any manager or said anything about how he ran the club. I was there to do what the manager told me to do, not to criticize anybody.

I knew I could still play, and it bothered me that people always brought up my age—37 at that time—and said that was an indication that I was over the hill. It was the same argument Ozzie Smith was to make when he was nearing the end of his career. He didn't want people using his age against him, noting that every player ages differently, and one guy could still be a great player at 37 when another guy was struggling. That was my point as well, and I think the Braves really were looking for an excuse to phase me out because they wanted to start going with younger players.

When I played so well in spring training and won the job, it messed up their plans. They had to wait for me to slip and struggle a little bit before they could start using my age against me and try to get me out of the lineup. I ended up playing only 68 games, hit .257 and we finished second, seven games behind the Pirates. It did not come as a surprise when the Braves released me following the season, and in a way I welcomed the news because it gave me a chance to make another fresh start.

Had I been convinced that I couldn't play or perform any more, I might have had a different attitude and gone ahead and retired. The way I had been used, or misused, by the Braves in 1960 only convinced me more that I needed to work harder to come back and show them and everybody else in the game that I could still play.

My old buddy, Bing Devine, had taken over as general manager of the Cardinals, and he knew I wanted to return home if it was possible. When he offered me a chance to come back to St. Louis, even if it wasn't a guaranteed contract, I took it. It gave me an extra incentive to go to spring training in 1961 and play well, so I could make the Cardinals' roster.

My former manager, Haney, who had taken the job as GM of the expansion Angels, called and offered me a contract to come with him to California and play second for his new club. It was a tempting offer, knowing I would have a job instead of hoping I would stick with the Cardinals, and I probably did think about it for a couple of minutes before I turned Fred down.

That was one of those decisions that, in hindsight, likely affected the rest of my life, certainly my baseball life. Had I taken the job with Haney and the Angels, I doubt if I ever would have played for the Cardinals again. Had I not played for the Cardinals, I probably would not have coached for the team and that meant I almost certainly would never have become the Cardinals' manager. We'll never know what would have happened had I gone to California instead.

Had St. Louis not been home, I might have gone. I also thought, however, that St. Louis was a good place for my family and for the kids to grow up. They were happy and comfortable, and I had enough confidence in my own ability to make the club that I really didn't think I was taking much of a risk in turning down the Angels contract.

Years later, when Fred died in 1977, his wife wrote me a letter. She said when she went through Fred's wallet, she found a $2 bill with my autograph. Fred had carried that in his wallet for a long time, thinking it was his good-luck charm. He had been managing Pittsburgh earlier in his career, and this was during a time when you couldn't get an alcoholic drink on Sunday. Fred had a little reserve that he kept with him, and I knew about it. One Sunday I told our clubhouse kid to go see Fred and ask him to pour me a drink, and I signed the $2 bill and sent it over to him as a joke. Fred came over with the drink and he kept that $2 bill until the day he died.

Coming back to the Cardinals reunited me with Musial, who was still blasting homers and playing terrific even after celebrating his 40th birthday. Sharing rides to the ballpark with Stan everyday was one of the benefits of being back in St. Louis, and we became inseparable again.

Bing and I had talked before working out my contract, and I knew the job he wanted me to do, come off the bench as a pinch-hitter and play occasionally in the field. That was fine with me, because I knew that was the arrangement coming in. When you know what your job is, and what the team wants you to do, it's much easier to prepare for that assignment, mentally and physically. The times players get upset is when they aren't informed about what the manager wants him to do, or when his situation changes without a logical explanation.

Pinch-hitting was something I really wasn't very familiar with, since I had been a starter almost all of my career. Since I knew that's what I would be doing, however, I accepted the role and prepared myself for it. It also helped that I had played the game as long as I had, it gave me a little more of an idea about when I might be used in the game. I kind of viewed it like being a relief pitcher. When my turn was coming, I would run up and down the steps leading to the clubhouse to loosen up, then I would swing the bat a little bit and I was ready to go.

There are some older players in the game who have a hard time adapting to a backup role. They are used to being stars and being in the limelight and it's hard for them to sit on the bench and let somebody else have the glory. Those are the kinds of players who should retire when they are on top, before their skills fade and they can't be every day players, and before they are remembered by fans as somebody who "hung on" too long and didn't know when it was time to quit.

For me, baseball had been my life and I wanted to stay involved in the game in some way when my playing career was over. That was why it didn't bother me to move into a backup, pinch-hitting role. I just looked it at as another stage of my career, getting me prepared to learn more about the game in case I got into coaching or managing.

Coming back to St. Louis also meant a return to my old number 2 uniform. It's funny how different players get known by their uniform numbers, and how they got that uniform in the first place. People who don't remember me from my playing days always assume I wore number 2 my entire career, but that wasn't true.

When I came up as a rookie in 1945 and Stan Musial was in the Navy, the clubhouse man, Butch Yatkeman, gave me Stan's number. I had never cared or worried about what number I had, so it didn't bother me. I guess at the time nobody knew Stan would become the greatest player in team history, so they didn't see the need to save his uniform number for him while he was in the service.

When Stan came back to play in 1946, I had to switch numbers, and Butch just handed me number 2. I didn't ask for it, and I don't know if there was any special reason he gave me that number. I did hit second in the order most of the time in those days, but if that was the reason, he never told me.

When I was traded to the Giants, I switched to number 7 and with the Braves I wore number 4. Getting number 2 back with the Cardinals really made it feel like I was coming home again.

Solly Hemus, one of my old double-play partners, was managing the Cardinals at the start of the 1961 season, but when the team struggled, Devine made a change in the middle of the season and replaced him with Johnny Keane.

Keane was an old-school kind of manager, in the sense that he wanted his players to be disciplined, to have sound fundamentals and to be well schooled in the knowledge of what to do in certain situations. He was a good teacher of the game, as you would expect from somebody who spent a long time managing in the minors, like he did. He enjoyed having good relationships with his players, but he wanted to be the boss, he wanted his players to respect him and to do what he told them. None of that was a problem for me.

Coming off the bench and being used in a reserve role, I improved my average that year to an even .300, playing in 72 games. I was ready to return to that same job in 1962, until I got a call one day shortly after the season from Devine and Keane.

They were determining which players they would have to keep from going to the two new expansion teams that were entering the league, the Mets and Houston Colt 45s, who later changed their name to the Astros. They had some good younger players they wanted to protect, which I could understand, and that didn't leave room for me. They said there were other teams that had expressed interest in me for the same job as I had filled with the Cardinals, and I really was thinking they were about to tell me I was being released when they brought up another possibility.

Devine and Keane offered me a chance to stay with the Cardinals as a coach if I didn't want to play for another team. If I signed a coaching contract instead of a playing contract, I wouldn't have to be protected and wouldn't be eligible to go to New York or Houston. It wasn't a hard decision, so I became a coach.

I didn't know exactly what my duties would be when I reported to spring training in February, and I'm not entirely certain if Keane did either. He told me to make certain I got plenty of batting practice, "just in case," and he used me in a lot of the spring training games.

Just as the regular season was about to begin, Keane told me I was being returned to the active playing roster.

Looking back on it, I wonder if that had been Devine and Keane's plan all along; to say I was going to be a coach and at the same time thinking they later would return me to the playing roster. I doubt it, I think it just worked out that way, but if I had been with the Mets or Houston and cared about it, I might have raised the issue at least. They didn't have some of the rules back then that they have now about the rosters and things like that, so I'm certain nobody thought twice about it.

At the time, Keane's explanation was simple.

I just don't know where you can pick up a player who can combine Red's know how and ability. He can't move as well as he used to, of course, but he can hit, and if necessary, fill in a few days at second base.

One thing I never realized until now was that the Redhead was as good hitting righthanded as he is lefthanded. He's the same as he is from the left side—a good line-drive hitter.

— *Johnny Keane*

Keane liked me because I did what was asked of me, never complained, and had some success in the role. Being a switch-hitter helped, because it made it harder on the opposing manager to know if he should put in a relief pitcher or not. I didn't strike out very often, I was a good situational hitter and didn't hit into many double plays.

I also learned how to pinch-hit, which is a skill that nobody can teach you. There is a strategy to that part of the game as much as there is to anything else. What I did, and what I later tried to tell my players who were going up to pinch-hit, was to go up to the plate swinging. Players who wait are giving the pitcher a chance to throw a free strike. The pitcher has enough of an advantage with the seven fielders behind him that hitters don't need to give themselves only two strikes instead of three.

Being reunited with Stan also made the last couple of years of my career a great experience. We no longer roomed together on the road because each of us had a private room, but we still hung out a lot together and sat around and talked about the game.

We both knew the end of our careers was coming, but we really wanted to make it back to the World Series one more time before we hung it up. After finishing sixth in 1962, we didn't know if we would have that chance.

The Cardinals decided they wanted me to become a coach in 1963. I worked with the infielders and sat with Keane on the bench, sometimes discussing strategy and possible moves, until late June when we got into a roster bind and I was activated.

I got into six games, making five pinch-hit appearances, but failed to get a hit. My final at-bat in the majors came on July 7, in the first game of a doubleheader in San Francisco. I came to bat in the 14th inning for Lou Burdette and grounded out.

The next day was the first day of the All-Star break, and the team put me on waivers, ending my career as a player, and returned me to the coaching staff.

The news wasn't earth-shattering. The *Globe-Democrat* ran a small story with the headline "Schoendienst Out As Player" but the *Post-Dispatch* reported the news in three short paragraphs. The story was covered in one paragraph in *The Sporting News.*

Keane said at the time he hadn't been able to play me enough to keep me sharp, but I just think it was time to make the move to the bench. I had reached my goal of playing until I was 40 and I was staying in the game and with the Cardinals, so I really didn't have much to complain about.

With six weeks to go in the season, Stan announced that 1963 also would be his final season as a player. His announcement was much more major news, with a big ceremony and the retirement of his No. 6, and that's what he deserved. He was leaving the game, and I was sticking around.

We put on a great stretch run in September, going 19-1 over one stretch, but couldn't quite catch the Dodgers. We got within one game before fading, finishing second, six games out.

Stan always said he had only one regret about his career, and it was almost the same as mine. He said he always wished he could have played in the majors with a healthy arm, thinking back to that day in the minors when he fell and hurt his arm. If he had indeed been truly healthy, he would have been an even more unbelievable player than he was.

Sitting on the bench more at the end of my career gave me more time to observe the game and notice things that sometimes I had taken for granted when I was playing everyday, like the umpires.

When I came up to the majors, there only were three umpires instead of four. That kept the base umpires more into the game, because they always had to be moving to cover the plays, but it also made their job a lot tougher. Having four umpires makes the responsibility different, and the one thing it should ensure is that the umpire always is in the right place to make the call on a play at his base.

Umpires have a tough job. They don't have the benefit of watching replays and looking at different angles to determine if a guy is safe or out or if a ball is fair or foul. They have to see it once and make a call. What replays have shown over the years is that they are correct a lot more often than they are wrong.

There are a lot of good guys in the umpiring ranks, and they really don't mind when a coach or a manager comes out to ask them about a call. They know sometimes the manager may realize it's the correct call, but he has to come out to protect his player from getting kicked out of the game or to show the home fans that he is working.

The best umpires have the same characteristics as the best players. they hustle and work hard. They bear down and give their best effort, and that's all you can ask. You can't lose your focus for a moment, because that might be the one moment you have to decide a play that will determine the outcome of the game.

Al Barlick always impressed me as being a great umpire. He didn't joke around with any of the players or managers, like some of the umpires try to do today, but he was serious about his job and he came out every day and worked hard, no matter if he was umpiring home plate or third base. He was an umpire who you could argue with, and that's important in a good umpire. He would let you present your case, actually listening to what you were saying, and then say, "That's enough," and you knew you had to get back in the dugout.

He didn't ever go out of his way to challenge a player or manager, as some guys do today. Umpires today seem too confrontational for me, and too willing to get in a player or manager's face and go toe-to-toe with them. The best umpires are the ones who give players a little space, who let them air their frustrations and disappointments—usually at themselves—and then get on with the game.

It's an old saying but it's true—if you go to a game and can't say afterward who the umpire was, he probably did a great job.

I don't think anybody who makes it to the majors is a bad umpire, but there are some who are better than others.

It's hard to evaluate umpires, but I think they need to have a better system where the ones who are consistently being challenged by players and umpires and consistently make mistakes could be weeded out. Umpires probably need to know more about what it's like to be a player, and players need to know more about what it's like to be an umpire.

When Frankie Frisch was managing in the late 1940s, umpire Beans Reardon was working a game one day on a brutally hot day. It would not have been unusual for Frisch to try to get himself kicked out of the game, so he could find a place to cool off. He was yelling at Reardon from the dugout, until Reardon finally called time and walked over to him. "You're going to stay here as long as I am today no matter what you say. I'm not going to throw you out."

Another time, we had a young player who was complaining about every call going against him, and Reardon turned to him and said, "I'm not going to throw you out. If I did it would help the club." The kid didn't say another word the rest of the year.

One of the best stories involving an umpire I ever heard concerned an umpire who was riding on a train from New York to Philadelphia. He had made a call in a game, and while he was on the train, another passenger recognized him. The guy didn't get on him or anything, but told the umpire, "I thought you missed that call today, out at second base." The umpire replied, "Well, I thought I got it right. I was right on top of the play. Where were you?"

The man said, "I was in the stands. It looked liked you missed it."

The umpire wasn't about to give up. "What do you do for a living?" he asked the guy. The man said, "I'm a judge." That was a great answer for the umpire, because it proved his point perfectly. "You've got all the time in the world. You've got months to make a decision. I have to make mine in a blink. You've got months. You can study your decisions."

The guy didn't say a word the rest of the trip. The umpires do have to make split-second decisions, and anybody who doesn't think it's tough should try it sometime. It really will change their way of thinking and they will learn to give the umpire a lot more credit than is normally the case.

The 1964 season was one of the most exciting in Cardinals' history as the team made a major trade, acquiring Lou Brock, fired GM Bing Devine, came back from a seemingly impossible 6 1/2 game margin with two weeks left to play and won the pennant, the first for the franchise since our title in 1946.

We would not have won the pennant had we not made the trade for Brock, getting him from the Cubs in a six-player deal on the June 15 trading deadline in what turned out to be the greatest deal in Cardinal history. We gave up Ernie Broglio, a good pitcher, and there actually were a lot of people who were upset by the trade, thinking the Cardinals had given up too much for the 25-year-old Brock.

The ballclub was in Houston, and Johnny Keane and Bing called in all of the coaches and asked us what we thought of Brock. My first comment was, "What do we have to give up?" Both Johnny and Bing snapped at me—don't worry about that, just tell us what you think of him. I said, "The little I've seen him play I can tell he's got a good arm, he can run." They wanted to know if he was a good outfielder, and I said he was playing right field in Wrigley Field, which is a tough job. I concluded that I liked him and thought he had a lot of plusses, depending on what we had to give up to get him. The two guys snapped at me again as I left the office. The next day we made the trade and he joined the ballclub.

In the old Houston stadium, you entered the dugout after coming into the field at the right field corner and I can still picture Lou walking toward the dugout, carrying his bats and glove over his shoulder. He stepped into the lineup and we were on our way.

Bing wasn't around to enjoy the success. Gussie got upset because of an incident that he didn't know about, and used it as a reason to get rid of Bing, publicly saying it was because the team hadn't won in such a long time. I felt sorry for Bing, because you never like to see anybody get fired or let go, but I really tried to keep to myself in those days and not get involved in other people's business. I was glad he landed on his feet with the Mets, and later on came back to the Cardinals again.

After we capped our comeback by winning the pennant on the final day of the season, we beat the Yankees in another seven-game World Series. The thrill and joy of victory had not really had time to sink in, however, before Johnny Keane stunned the city with the news that he was resigning as manager of the Cardinals.

It turned out Keane had heard about Busch being dissatisfied with him, even before Busch fired Devine, and he knew Busch was plotting with Leo Durocher about taking over as the manager. Even before we won the pennant and the World Series, Keane had written his letter of resignation and was waiting to present it to Busch.

I was sorry to see Johnny leave, because I enjoyed working for him and I thought he was a quality person and manager. Also, I had no idea what it would mean for my future, since almost any manager gets a free hand in picking his own coaching staff. If the rumors about Durocher were correct, I didn't think my future was going to be in St. Louis. When Keane suddenly signed on to manage the Yankees just four days after leaving the Cardinals, I wondered if maybe he would want to take me with him.

I didn't have to wait long to get my answer.

Chapter 9

THE MANAGER

J ust a few days after the end of the World Series and Keane's resignation, some of the people who worked for Mr. Busch with the brewery and the ballclub invited me out to help them train some dogs for hunting pheasants and ducks.

One of the men who was there was Ollie Von Gontard, who was related to Gussie, and he had come from a meeting where the ballclub executives were talking about who they should hire as manager.

"You know you're being considered," he told me.

I didn't know it, but I was pleased someone had put my name in the hopper. I never had really thought about managing, but I knew I wanted to stay in the game for a long time and I guess realistically it was a natural progression.

Bob Howsam was the general manager, having replaced Bing Devine, and I got word later that morning that he and Mr. Busch were looking for me. I was supposed to attend a meeting with Joe Linneman at the Mari de Villa retirement home we had built.

I returned the call to Mr. Busch, who said he wanted to meet with me. We arranged a time for the next day, and I went to the ballpark and spent time with Gussie and Bob Howsam. I spent close to an hour with Howsam, who was asking all kinds of technical questions about what I would do in certain situations if I was the manager, about what kinds of trades I thought the club should make and other personnel evaluations.

He suddenly jumped up from his chair and asked how I would like to manage. I said that would be great, and he said, "You're my new manager."

It happened so quickly, I really didn't have time to think about it. Johnny's resignation was announced on October 16, and the news conference introducing me as the new manager was held four days later. I had to cancel a goose-hunting trip so I could be at the news conference.

A committee had been appointed to make recommendations about who should be the new manager, and Stan Musial was one of the people on the committee. Howsam was said to be campaigning for Charlie Metro, who had managed for him in the minors, and former Cardinal Alvin Dark was another name that was brought up.

With Musial leading my support, it came down to as much a public relations decision as a baseball one, I think, and that's where I had the advantage. There was a lot of negative reaction to Johnny leaving, and the possible hiring of Durocher had stirred up a lot of people. The prevailing thought was the new manager needed to be someone who was a favorite of the fans, and luckily that turned out to be me.

The team's brass really was taking a chance on me, however. I was 41 years old, had never managed before, and had only been a coach for two seasons. I felt comfortable that I could do the job, however, and was ready to put my full-time energy and devotion into the post.

Stepping in to manage a team that had just won the World Series was not an easy task. Only once before had a team changed managers after winning the World Series, and that had been the Cardinals again, in 1926, when owner Sam Breadon had traded Rogers Hornsby to the Giants for Frankie Frisch when they had gotten locked in a bitter contract dispute.

That immediately puts pressure on you, because the fans want you to win again, and it's hard to do that in any circumstance. It was even harder in our situation, because we were going into 1965 with a lot of veteran players who were on the downside of their careers.

As a new manager, you would prefer to take over an up-and-coming club loaded with good young players who are coming into the prime of their careers. With the Cardinals that year, we had players like Dick Groat, Ken Boyer, Bill White and Curt Simmons who had all been great players, but were headed toward the end of their careers. You couldn't expect them to play again at the same level, and that was going to make it hard for the team to succeed.

Fans sometimes have a hard time understanding nuances of the game like that. To them it was a case of "you won last year with these players, why can't you win again?"

An early indication of what my rookie managerial season was going to be like came one Sunday when we were playing in Cincinnati. We were limping along in 10th place, and I had to walk to Mass because the cab drivers were on strike. I already had a cold, and then got caught in a cloudburst and got drenched. When I reached the clubhouse at Crosley Field and changed into my uniform, I went out to the dugout and got caught again under a leaky roof. After the game, as we headed for Milwaukee, a hot cup of coffee spilled in my lap and went all over my suit.

As a player, I knew all about the ups and downs in the game, so the down times never bothered me too much, and I was determined to be that way as a manager as well. I didn't want to get too high when we won or start throwing things and upending the buffet table if we lost, but I did get frustrated a lot that season.

I never was worried about my job security, even though I had a one-year contract and we were headed to a seventh-place finish, one game below .500. I was confident in my abilities as a manager, and I thought Gussie would stick with me longer than one year, no matter how bad things were.

After a game at home in September, one of the men who worked for Gussie came down to the manager's office and said, "The boss would like to see you in the Roost," which is where he watched the games, a little suite up near the roof. He told me to come the way I was, but I said I had to take a shower and change first. When I got up to the Roost, Gussie and some other guys were playing gin rummy. Gussie stopped the game and came over and we talked for about 15 or 20 minutes.

Finally he said, "Well I'm going to have you back. What would it take to have you back?" I remember saying, "Boss, we didn't have a good year, so what can I say? I can't ask for any money or anything. You asked me to come back, and I'm just happy to come back and we'll just leave it at that."

Maybe I should have asked for something, like stock or something. He might have given it to me. As it was, I was just grateful to get another shot the following year, and I wound up signing for the same amount of money I had signed for the previous year.

I learned a lot about managing in that first season, lessons I was to apply the rest of the time I had the job. I learned about setting rules, and letting the players know who was the boss. I learned about developing my managerial philosophy, and how to build a good relationship with my players.

Most of what I learned about managing came in bits and pieces from all of the managers I had played for, and I wanted to be a combination of most of those guys. Fred Haney, to me, seemed to have the best relationship with his players and that was the kind of manager I tried to be.

I learned as a player that the most important thing you want from a manager is communication. You don't want to be left in the dark, wondering why you weren't playing, what role the manager had in mind for you, and things like that. As a player, you want a manager who will tell you those things and not leave you guessing.

As long as my players gave 100 percent effort all the time, I had no room to complain about them. I also knew as a player that you didn't like it when you were shown up by the manager. I vowed never to do that. If I had a problem with a player, we discussed it face-to-face, not in front of the entire team. I always tried to put my players in a position where they had the best chance of success, and not ask them to do things they weren't capable of. That, to me, is a mistake a lot of inexperienced managers make. They either ask their players to do unrealistic things or they don't know enough about a player's strengths and weaknesses to figure out the best way to use him.

The most important skill a manager can have is a thorough knowledge of his players. You have to do the things your players can do, whether it is the way you personally prefer to play or not. If a guy was a good hit-and-run man, you hit-and-ran with him. If a player had other strengths, that's what you did. I don't think you can tell players they have to do certain things one particular way. Everybody has his own way of playing the game.

People also talk about managers making rules for the team, but the players are the ones who set the rules. I really only asked my players to do two things, to be on time and to give 100 percent. There were times I had to fine guys, but nobody ever knew about it.

I never got on players for making errors, and there is a difference between an error and a mistake. Throwing to the wrong base is a mistake. Booting a ground ball is an error. I talked to the players after they made a mistake, making certain they knew what they had done wrong, trying to ensure that it could not happen again. Physical errors are part of the game and the managers and players have to realize that.

As the manager, you never could get in a situation where you let a player take advantage of you, or let a player embarrass himself or the club. It all comes back to communicating, and if the manager makes all of those points clear to his players, there shouldn't be any problems.

Organization is another important skill for a manager. You have to know who you have available on the bench and in the bullpen, and have an idea ahead of time about what you are going to do if a certain situation comes up. A manager never wants to be surprised or caught off guard by something, because the players will be able to sense that he was not prepared and they will start to lose confidence in him.

Mary learned what it was like to be the wife of a manager, too. She took it upon herself to become a tutor and unofficial advisor to the players' wives as well, and that was a role she enjoyed. Someone asked her to write down her thoughts on what it was like to be a baseball player's wife, and this is what she wrote:

She's a new bride
She's usually thin.
She probably grew up with her ballplayer husband, or met him at school or on a blind date.
She's a very good driver.
You may detect a little bit of loneliness in her because her husband is away a great part of the time.
She's efficient and self-reliant.
She's happy, gay, sad, worrisome and nervous.
She may have been a model, airline hostess, school teacher, nurse.
She often has a college degree.
She's always looking for a babysitter.
She's from any part of the country.
She loves going to Florida and spring training.
She's a whiz at packing a suitcase and driving across country with a new baby.
She can come up from the minor leagues on Tuesday night and be at the ballpark in the majors on Wednesday night.
She spends half of her time waiting for her famous husband either at the ballpark or airport.
She adores an off night, which seldom occurs.
She not only watches major league baseball but Little League games also.
Her husband's hobby in all probability is hunting, fishing or golfing. They both love music. She loves to dance.
He loves football, live or TV.
Sheer joy for a pitcher's wife—a shutout. An outfielder's wife—a 4-for-4 night. An infielder's wife—a sensational stop that's turned into a double play. A catcher's wife—throwing the runner out at second. Ecstacy—a home run.
She spends birthdays, anniversaries usually without her husband.
She knows all about autographs, radio announcers, fan mail, sports writers and leaving men on base.
She wears a baseball charm bracelet.

Her first baby usually is a girl.
She does not keep score.
She's used to traveling, crowds, diapers, extra innings, furnished apartments and hot dogs.
She dies when her husband strikes out.
She struggles with the children at the ballgame.
She struggles with the children at home.
She struggles with the children at the airports.
She struggles with the children on car trips, plane trips, in hotels, in motels, at grocery stories, during batting slumps.
She's almost sure her husband will have to go to a luncheon, or banquet or work out on an off day.
She cuts pictures out of the newspapers and makes scrap books.
She waits for long distance phone calls.
She has a son who has a baseball uniform just like his father's.
She comes to know she can never have a routine or normal life, but she loves every minute of the exciting and thrilling life of a ballplayer's wife, and she prays every day her husband will stay healthy, do his job well on the field, win the game that day and then come home to a few happy hours with her alone.
Oh yes, She knows that the best managers have red hair.
—Mary Schoendienst

When I managed, we didn't have all of the computer printouts and charts and data that are available to managers today. I think some of the guys rely too much on all that stuff, going strictly by the numbers and "by the book" and never taking a chance or a gamble on a gut feeling. If baseball was meant to be played strictly by the numbers and "by the book" you could let a computer tell you what moves to make and you wouldn't even need the manager.

Baseball is still a people game, and managers have to remember that. You are managing people, not machines. Most managers understand that, and they also understand a very basic rule—the better your players, the more games you are going to win. The best manager in the world isn't going to win the pennant if he doesn't have any quality players, and the worst manager in the world is going to have to try awfully hard to mess up a team that is loaded with gifted players.

Another lesson I learned early was that a manager's other responsibility is to the press. The coverage of the team had changed since I played, when there were a lot of newspapers, no television reporters or cameras and the only radio guys around were the team play-by-play broadcasters.

The coming of television changed the way the newspaper reporters went about their job, forcing them to go beyond the play-by-play details of the game. Because they had to write more analytical and interpretive stories, they had to come down and talk to the manager and players more often and get our opinions on issues and what had happened during the game.

I always had a good relationship with the press. We had two newspapers that covered all of our games, the *Post-Dispatch* and the *Globe-Democrat*, and the writers there were good guys who understood the game and never were critical unless it was deserved. I just wanted the coverage to be fair, and if it was—even if it was negative—there wasn't anything I could complain about.

We were fortunate in St. Louis to have two first-class guys running the sports sections of the *Post* and *Globe*, Bob Broeg and Bob Burnes, who provided good coverage and were good guys. They didn't go around trashing players and writing critical and negative stories like you might have found in some other cities.

One writer who always impressed me was Arthur Daley of the *New York Times*. Whenever he wanted an interview with you, he would call and arrange it a day ahead of time. It wasn't like today where writers just barge in on you and expect you to drop whatever you're doing and talk to them.

It also was important to have a good relationship with the team's broadcasters, because what they say about your team can go a long way in shaping the way the fans think about you and the job you are doing. Even though the broadcaster should be objective, he can really slant the facts to make it seem like things are going good or bad.

Harry Caray began broadcasting the Cardinals' games in 1945, the same year I broke into the majors. He was still the main play-by-play broadcaster when I became the manager, and we always got along well. We would go to dinner occasionally when the team was on the road, and even though I never heard his broadcasts because I was in the dugout, I think he was fair in what he said.

I know there were players he was critical of and some he treated harsher than others, but that's going to happen. Not everybody on a team is going to be buddy-buddy, so you can't expect the broadcaster to like everybody on the team either. As far as I know Harry always was fair to me.

Harry got fired after the 1969 season—I never asked why or tried to get more information about it—and then Jack Buck, who had been working with Harry for a long time, took over as the main announcer. He and I became great friends, because we were about the same age and had a lot of the same interests, like going to nice restaurants and the shows when we were on the road.

Jack is easy to be around, and one regret I had was that I never got to listen to his broadcasts. I know he's a great announcer, but I always was on the field or in the dugout. I did get to listen to him on football games, and he always did a great job in that sport as well.

Jack was a great interviewer, and he made all of the shows we did so easy. He knew what questions to ask, and part of the reason was that he knew the game. He knew why some moves worked and others didn't, and he knew when to question a manager's strategy.

As far as I know, Jack always said nice things about me, but then he could have ripped me and I wouldn't have heard it— but I think somebody would have been listening and would have told me about it.

Another reason Jack stood apart from the rest of the broadcasters was he possessed another unique skill—he listened when somebody was talking. A lot of guys will have all of their questions planned out in advance, no matter what your answers are, and that results in a bad interview. Jack never did that—he waited and listened to what you had to say, then asked an intelligent follow-up question.

One of the fun things about being with Jack was we always were running into somebody that he knew. He was like Musial in the sense that he had done so many things and met so many interesting people in his life that no matter where we were or what we were doing, one of them was bound to show up.

Jack always tried to be positive on his broadcasts, and that's something else I don't think all announcers do. There's a difference between being positive and being a homer, and Jack definitely wasn't a homer. I know he probably had some bad things to say about our team during the 1965 season, but he wasn't the only one who had those thoughts. The bad year prompted a couple of deals just after the season was over.

First, Howsam sent our captain and the World Series star of the previous year, Boyer, to the Mets for Charley Smith and Al Jackson. A week later, we traded Groat, White and Bob Uecker to the Phillies for Pat Corrales, Art Mahaffey and Alex Johnson.

Neither trade worked out as well as we had hoped, and the 1966 season hadn't started out well when Howsam swung a deal with San Francisco that was to be a key to our success in coming seasons. On the day we closed the old Busch Stadium and prepared to move to the new ballpark downtown, we acquired Orlando Cepeda from the Giants for Ray Sadecki.

We needed a first baseman, since we really hadn't replaced White, and we had a meeting to discuss the trade with Howsam, Musial and myself. Howsam wasn't certain he should make the deal, but I told him I thought we had enough pitching that we could afford to give up Sadecki. He was still hemming and hawing, and a day later we got together again and started talking. Finally Stan spoke up and said, "Either you make the deal or you don't. Red would like to make the deal." That's when the trade was made.

We won three more games in 1966 than we had the year before, but I thought we were making the changes necessary to make us a better team. Because Smith had not worked out the way we had hoped, we really only had one hole to fill, at third base. As we looked at ways to improve the club over the winter, the possibility came up that if we could acquire an outfielder, perhaps we could move Mike Shannon to third base. That became a reality in December when he we traded Smith to the Yankees for Roger Maris.

Some critics didn't think Shannon would be able to play third base, but I knew Mike well enough to believe he could do it. Joe Schultz, our third base coach, and I spent a lot of time that winter working with him on playing third base. The football Cardinals still were in St. Louis, and we would work out next to them at the ballpark, hitting him ground balls by the dozen. It was cold out there, and we even took him to Forest Park and worked out there.

I knew Mike was a tough enough guy that he could do the job. If nothing else, he would get in front of the ball and knock in down with his chest. Before going to spring training, I thought he had made enough progress to keep the experiment going because I really thought it was going to make us a much stronger club. I really didn't know who would play third if Shannon had not been able to do it.

In Florida, George Kissell and I worked with Mike every day. Kissell would pitch to me, and I would bat both righthanded and lefthanded and hit balls to Shannon. I would pull the ball and slice it to him. I bunted it, and we studied different situations so he would know what to do. One day somebody counted and I hit him more than 200 balls. Another day he fielded more than 200 bunts.

Mike was quoted at the time as saying how awful it was and that he kept thinking he was messing up. He was learning though, and that was the important thing. I wanted him to get used to everything he had to do, and he didn't back down one bit.

His being able to make the switch to third base cemented the lineup, because it gave us a veteran player at every position who knew what to do and how to play the game. As a manager, it was pretty much of a dream team because I had to do very little managing. I filled out the lineup card, told the guys to go play and then sat back and watched.

Stan had taken over as general manager for Howsam, who took a job with the Reds, and we made only three minor roster moves the entire season, which would be unheard of today. The only player we acquired during the season was relief pitcher Jack Lamabe, from the Mets in exchange for Al Jackson.

We never even looked at the waiver wire, because Stan's opinion was that if a guy wasn't good enough for another ballclub, he wasn't good enough for us. We didn't need any help that year, fortunately, and were never challenged after moving into first place in June. We clinched the pennant on September 18, ended up with 101 victories and finished with a 10 1/2 game margin on second-place San Francisco.

I know you would get a challenge from some people, but I believe the regular lineup of that team was about as good a team as you could put together.

Cepeda played first, and he became the first player in history to earn unanimous selection as the league MVP. When we got him from the Giants, Herman Franks was their manager and he told me that Cepeda would be a good player and play like heck for us, and he did.

At second base we had Julian Javier, and there wasn't much I needed to tell him because he knew how to play. Jack Buck asked me one time during an interview what I was going to say to Javier about playing second, since that was my old position. I told Jack the only thing I needed to tell Hoolie was that I wanted him to be the relay man on balls hit to the outfield because he had such a good arm.

Dal Maxvill had taken over for Groat, who had been a great player for us in the early 1960s. Dick always was somebody I thought would stay in the game, perhaps as a manager, but he never did. He was a good player, and a tough player, and he would have made a good manager had that been the direction he chose after his playing career.

In Maxvill, we had a shortstop who wasn't a great hitter, but he always seemed to come up with big hits at big times. He knew how to win, that was his biggest attribute. He made the big plays at the critical moments in games. You see a lot of players make plays when their team either is getting beat by a big margin or way ahead, but the players I wanted on my team were the ones who could make the big plays when the game was tied or a one or two-run margin. Maxie was that kind of player. You won with guys like that on your team.

I had been sorry to see Boyer go when we made that deal, because he was such a solid player who always just did his job and never was flashy or a showman. He had a good career, and I think he really should have received more consideration for the Hall of Fame when you look at his final career numbers. Moving him, even though Smith didn't work out as his replacement in 1966, opened the way for us to move Shannon to third the following year.

Mike was a tough player. He wanted to play, and he was the kind of guy you couldn't blast out of the lineup with a sledgehammer.

The catalyst to our ballclub was Lou Brock, the leadoff hitter and leftfielder. People always thought of him as a basestealer above everything else, and a lot of people didn't realize how strong he was. He was the kind of player who made things happen when he reached base, because he forced the other team to think about him because they knew he was going to run and try to steal second. He brought a lot of excitement to our team and the game.

Curt Flood played center and usually batted behind Brock. He did everything you wanted a second-place hitter to do, handling the bat well and being able to hit to the opposite field. He understood the game very well and knew what he needed to do in every situation. If he saw the third baseman playing way back of the bag, he knew to lay the ball down. I didn't have to give him a sign. He knew what he was doing.

Maris was in right, and he was a pleasure to be around and have on the team. I think he was so happy to be out of New York and that pressure cooker that he would have done anything we asked of him. The only thing he ever told me that he didn't want to do was play left field, because he said he really had trouble picking up the ball off the bat from that angle. That was no problem for me, and he played right field very well.

Ever since breaking Babe Ruth's home run record, Maris had been in the spotlight in New York. When we made the deal for him, the one thing I told the St. Louis writers was that I hoped they wouldn't put that kind of pressure on him. I said he was coming to a different park, on a different team, in a different league and not to expect him to be a major home-run hitter.

Maris only hit nine homers for us in 1967, but he was a very valuable player. The press did lay off him, and Roger later thanked me for what I said because he said it was something he was worried about coming to a new town.

Tim McCarver was our regular catcher, and he knew what he was doing. It's very encouraging for a manager to have a veteran catcher who knows the game and his pitching staff, and we had that with Tim. He didn't have a great arm, but he got rid of the ball in a hurry. He was very focused when he was on the field and he was into the game from start to finish, no matter if it was a blowout or a nailbitter.

The pitching staff was led by Bob Gibson, who showed how tough he was when he stayed in a game even after a line drive off the bat of Roberto Clemente broke his leg. He missed two months, but was back for the World Series. There was no way anybody or any injury was going to keep him from pitching. A lot of times people would ask Gibson how he felt and he'd say, "I hurt all over, but I'm going to pitch."

Gibson was among the most competitive people I've ever been around. A lot of players on other teams tried to get him to talk to them, when they would be standing around the cage during batting practice, but Gibson wouldn't do it. He never said anything to anybody. He just went out and played.

Our opponent in the 1967 World Series was the Boston Red Sox, who didn't clinch the American League pennant until the final day of the season.

The national showcase was a coming-out party for Brock and Gibson, who played great as we edged the Red Sox in seven games. Brock hit .414 and stole a record seven bases, and Gibson won three games, including Game Seven.

The decision to bring Gibson back and start the seventh game on just two days' rest didn't seem like a smart one to some people. I received a lot of telegrams and well-wishes during the series, but one I received from a fan in California had a different message:

"It is none of my business," the telegram began, "You are a very fine manager, however, being an ex-high school catcher I cannot understand your reasoning for pitching Gibson tomorrow. If the

Cards have lost today I would understand your pitching choice. Busch Stadium is not like Fenway Park. Why take the chance and use Gibson after only two days' rest? It seems to me the Boston pitchers are all worn out. You're the boss, you're the manager, I hope you are right. I have nothing to lose on the series. God bless you and the rest of the Cards. Best regards."

At least Gibson was able to shut the guy up. His victory capped off what had been a great year for the team, not only because we won, but there just was such a great feeling among everybody who worked for the club. Working with Stan as the GM set the tone for the relationships that everybody on the club enjoyed.

At the time, Stan had some complimentary things to say about me which I really appreciated.

I know that he says he doesn't worry. I say that he does, but he's wise enough not to show it, which is most important in keeping the players from pressing or tensing. This was a loose, relaxed ballclub.

Red doesn't overmanage, doesn't try to fancy up too much a basically simple game. He doesn't try to outmaneuver the other side for maneuvering's sake. He doesn't overdo the hit-and-run or ask any player to employ a skill the player doesn't have.

It was tough on Red, having to start managing in the majors, but he has learned how to handle men, when to give them a rest and when to take out his pitchers.

He's sound and stable and makes the percentage move. He doesn't get excited and he doesn't feed anybody a lot of baloney. He's the (Walter) Alston type and should manage a long time.

— Stan Musial

The only time I remember being upset about the way the club was playing that year was once early in the season. I was getting ready to mow my yard, and pulled the cord so hard that it broke. Maybe it was just an old cord.

More typical of the good times that we enjoyed that season

was the night in Atlanta when we were all on the bus after a game, ready for the short ride back to the hotel, and no one could find the bus driver.

Everyone was getting restless, and finally one of our relief pitchers, Joe Hoerner, got up from where he was sitting, came and sat down in the driver's seat. He was going to drive that bus back to the hotel, but first he had to find out where the start button was.

He drove that bus through the tunnels and back to the hotel, and the only problem he had was hitting a street sign just as he pulled into the hotel. He parked the bus, and Leo Ward, our traveling secretary, called the company and told them they could come pick up their bus at the hotel.

Mary sometimes got upset with me because I didn't talk more at home about what was going on with the team, but I was from the old school, where we didn't advertise what was going on in the clubhouse.

I would know more by reading the newspaper. Red would never tell me anything. I was so mad at him because he never told me what was going on. I wanted him to give me some strategy and he never did. I had to learn baseball through my girls when they played.

— *Mary Schoendienst*

The team made a postseason trip to Japan, and that was very enjoyable. The people in Japan were really just starting to move into playing big-time baseball, and no matter where we went on the trip, I was surrounded by reporters wanting to know everything they could about the game.

We played a series of games around the country, and when we first got to Japan, it had been about 10 days since we had played. We had a couple of days available to practice and get loosened up, but it was raining so we couldn't work out.

We got beat in the first two games, and the press was all over us —how could the World Champions be losing to a Japanese team? I tried to explain to the reporters that we had not played any games for a while and weren't ready, and that I didn't want to take any chances on getting anybody hurt, but that was a hard explanation for them to accept. They kept asking, and it started to get on my nerves.

After the second game, I called a team meeting and said, "I think we're in good enough shape now that we can beat these guys. It's not club against club anymore. It's country against country. Now let's go play." We didn't lose another game the rest of the trip.

A lot of the Japanese players were trying to ask advice and learn as much as they could, and there was one little lefthanded pitcher who was trying to learn how to throw a changeup. We spent a day working with the Japanese players, and he got a lot of tips from our coaches. We had beaten up on him already in the trip, but then when we faced him again it was like he was a different pitcher. I learned the Japanese are very astute people, and it seemed every time we started talking their ears got bigger. They wanted to know everything so they could better themselves.

We got to do a lot of sightseeing as well, including going to Hiroshima. All of the Japanese reporters knew I had been in the military during World War II and that my brothers had been in the service, so I was asked what I thought when we were touring the site of the atomic bomb explosion.

It was bad. There wasn't much I could say, except that I hoped it wouldn't happen again. That seemed to be what the reporters wanted me to say.

We had a lot of formal dinners, and most of them were served in traditional Japanese style, meaning all of the guests took off their shoes and sat on the floor and ate on a very low table. That was OK for a while but then it started getting old.

Finally one day Musial said to one of our hosts, "I think there ought to be a time somewhere where we don't have to sit on the floor for dinner. It's getting expensive keeping the women in nylons because they keep popping them." The next night we went to a restaurant where we didn't have to sit on the floor.

We met a lot of nice people and became friends with some, including the man who owned the Coca-Cola distributorship. Stan and I became good friends with him, and he even came to the United States in 1997—30 years later—and Stan and Lill joined Mary and me and we all went out to dinner.

Al Barlick, an umpire whom I had high regard for, was with us on the trip. I don't think they'd let players and an umpire travel together today, and that's probably a good thing.

I tried to never get into arguments or confrontations with umpires, but once in a while you had to do it to come out and protect your player and try to keep him out of trouble.

I was kicked out of two games while I was managing, and neither time was my fault. The first time came when Bill White hit a ground ball, and the umpire called him out at first base on a double play. It wasn't even close. I jumped out of the dugout and before I even got to the umpire, he tossed me. Before I could even question him about the call, I had to ask why he had thrown me out. "You're charging me," he said. I was still 50 yards away from him.

The only other ejection of my managing career came in Cincinnati. Shannon was called out on a play at the plate, and he jumped up and started arguing. I couldn't tell from where I was whether he was safe or out, but I went out to try to keep him in the game. We were losing the game by a pretty big score. I don't know why I did it, but while I was arguing with the umpire I backed up and re-enacted the slide into home.

The umpire laughed and said, "You know you can't do that, Red." I said, "I know that. We're getting beat pretty bad. I'll take a walk."

Later, I was talking with that darned Shannon about the play, and he told me he was out. My whole argument and slide demonstration was for nothing.

There weren't very many occasions for me to get upset with umpires or anybody else in 1968. We had almost the exact same team intact from the previous year, and even though Stan resigned as general manager, Mr. Busch brought back Bing Devine from the Mets, so I still had somebody in the office who was a good friend and someone I trusted and worked well with.

The players went about their business on the field, and led by Gibson's record-setting year, we were 15 games in front by August 1 and coasted to the pennant by a nine-game margin. Waiting for us in the World Series was the Detroit Tigers.

Behind Gibson's 17 strikeouts in Game One, we jumped on the Tigers and built a 3-1 lead. One more win would have given us consecutive World Championships, but that win didn't come. A break here or there might have made the difference, but the breaks went the way of the Tigers, and they won the Series.

Joe and Babe Linneman had gone with us and some other friends to Detroit, and Joe had taken a cartoon that Amadee, my friend who drew cartoons for the *Post-Dispatch*, had drawn and turned it into a billboard. It had a picture of a tiger hanging by his tail with a Redbird standing over it.

> *I had it on each side of a billboard and put it on a stick. I started in leftfield and walked through the ballpark. My brother-in-law was behind me, and the fans were really letting us have it. The next morning we were pictured on the front page of the newspaper with a guy trying to throw a cup of coffee on my head.*
>
> *They actually stopped the game because the fans were so riled up, and Red told me later he looked up from the dugout and said, "I know that's that old SOB Linneman." Mary said, "Joe you could have gotten killed." I didn't think they were going to get that upset.*
>
> *— Joe Linneman*

As it turned out, the Tigers' fans had the last laugh because of Detroit's comeback. Everybody in our clubhouse was upset and disappointed, but nobody knew then that it was going to be our final chance at a World Series for a long time. Everybody thought we would be just as competitive the next season as well, but it didn't happen.

Winning those two pennants meant I got to manage the NL All-Star team in 1968 and 1969, and those were enjoyable assignments. I wanted to win the games, and we did, but I also wanted to get everybody into the game if at all possible. Players say they don't care if they don't play in the game or not, but they do. It's their chance to be on television and stand out in front of their family and relatives, and if you are selected for the game you deserve a chance to play.

The only guy I didn't get into the first game, in Houston, was Gibson. He was tired and his arm was sore, so I tried not to use him if at all possible. The 1969 game was in Washington, and we built a big lead as Willie McCovey hit two home runs. All I was thinking about was getting everybody in, and I wasn't thinking about McCovey. I brought in somebody to take his place, and later I found out he could have broken a record if I had left him in the game. I felt bad about it and went over to apologize to him, but he wasn't upset.

The beauty of the All-Star game was getting to spend some time with guys like McCovey and the stars of other teams. Watching them up close made you truly appreciate how talented the stars were.

I always enjoyed being around guys who were truly happy to be in the major leagues. There were some guys when I played and managed—there are more today—who didn't comprehend how special a place it was and how much an honor it was to play baseball for a living.

I would rather be associated with a bunch of great guys, only ordinary players, who understand how lucky they are than have a team full of stars who were spoiled brats.

One of the people I enjoyed being around when I was managing was George Kissell, who first put on a Cardinal uniform in 1940 and hasn't taken it off yet. George has taught more people how to play baseball—the correct way—than anybody can count. That was what he used to do, teach school, in his hometown of Watertown, New York.

George played in the minor leagues for 10 years, and from 1946 to 1968 worked in the minor leagues in a variety of capacities. When we had an opening on the major-league coaching staff in 1969, I thought all of that dedication and work should be rewarded, so we promoted George to the majors.

There were people who questioned me about the decision, wondering if George could coach third. George had been coaching third along with doing everything else in the minors all those years. I had no doubts he could coach and be very successful in the majors. Even he was a little nervous, but I told him he could do it, and if it didn't work out, we could always move him to first base.

He stayed with me for the next six seasons, as long as I remained the manager, and he did a good job. He was always teaching, giving instruction to the players, and those who sat and listened and asked questions received a great education. Players like Ted Simmons and Joe Torre were always there, and I think the fact they have gone on to successful careers in front-office and managing positions is based at least in part on the things they learned from George.

Despite his success in the majors, and I was glad he stayed long enough to earn his pension, George's true calling in life is working with the kids, treating them as a father figure. A lot of the kids he works with in spring training, rookie ball and Class A ball have never been away from home before, living on their own, and George really looks after those guys and makes certain they stay out of trouble and don't run into problems.

The biggest problem we had in 1969 and the early years of the 1970s was trying to win games. The teams that had been so successful in 1967 and 1968 were getting older, and changes had to be made. Flood got into a contract dispute with Mr. Busch, and was traded to the Phillies. He refused to report, challenging the antitrust laws, and took his case all the way to the U.S. Supreme Court. Even though he ultimately lost, his efforts led the way for free agency a few years later.

We acquired Richie Allen in the Flood trade, and he was a good player for the Cardinals. It was hard for righthanded hitters at that time to hit the ball to right center with any authority, and he could do it. He had a reputation of being a difficult player, but he played hard for me. The only problem I had with him, and it was true throughout his career, is that he never seemed to play the last month of the season. He was always hurt or something was wrong.

It never bothered me as a manager if a player had a bad reputation or was known to cause problems on other teams. I judged him only by the way he played for me and the effort he put in when he was playing. As long as the player gave me 100 percent effort and didn't get into trouble off the field, that was good enough for me.

Richie always has remained friendly with me, and the last time I saw him in Philadelphia, he and his wife were in Bookbinder's Restaurant. He came over to our table and we had a nice, long conversation.

Richie was different than a lot of players, and that's not meant to be a derogatory comment. He played at a real confusing time for a lot of players, and there were guys who weren't certain exactly what they were supposed to do or how they were supposed to act. Guys the same age as major leaguers were going to fight in Vietnam, were starting to experiment with drugs, were involved in the civil rights movement, and it was only natural that the players were interested in all of those activities, just like the rest of society.

The biggest change I noticed was a change in attitude among the players. It probably was caused by all of those societal developments as well as the coming of free agency, but it made a manager's job much harder. When you asked a player to do something, there were guys who wanted to know why, and you didn't have the automatic power and authority that a manager was used to having.

The word that seemed to be forgotten, and still is forgotten today, is discipline. It's forgotten in every phase of life, in school, in baseball, everything. You've got to discipline yourself, and if you don't have it you're going to drift. It got harder to discipline players in the 1970s, just like it got harder to discipline your kids. You had better not say anything rough to any kid today, even if it's your own.

Everybody was wearing blue jeans at the time, that was the "in" thing. One time I ran into Milton Berle at the airport and he was decked out in blue jeans and a blue jean jacket. I asked him what he was doing wearing that outfit, and he said, "This cost a lot of money."

I never could get away from remembering the days I wore blue jeans as a kid growing up in Germantown. To me they represented nothing but work. When I wore blue jeans I was working on a farm from 4 a.m. until 10 o'clock in the evening. There was no way I could wear a pair of blue jeans once I got away from Germantown and off the farms. I've never had a pair of blue jeans since and there's no way I would.

The attitude of the players was accompanied by the increasing power of the union, led by Marvin Miller, which led to the first strike by the players in 1972. The game is still affected by labor problems that began then, and it could have been avoided. The owners caved in too quickly. The union wasn't as powerful back then as it is today, and if the owners had waited another week, they could have won that first battle and set a different tone for future labor negotiations.

Mary was upset by the strike for a different reason than the future of the game.

> *Mr. Busch had asked me to sing the National Anthem before the season opener. Our daughter Cathleen was in school in Rome, and we had gone there during the winter. I had bought a red, white and blue wool dress that I was going to wear to that game. I was ready, and then the players went on strike. I was furious, and Mr. Busch was so mad at them that even when the strike ended after a few days, he canceled the opening ceremonies. I lost my chance to sing at the opening game, but I did get more chances later and I did get opportunities to wear that dress.*
> *— Mary Schoendienst*

We had problems in other areas off the field as well. On a trip to Philadelphia in 1970, the hotel where we were staying caught fire in the early morning hours.

I was asleep, and the sirens woke me up. I could see the red lights flickering in my window. That was all I needed to get me going. I threw on a pair of pants and a shirt and hightailed it downstairs. I wasn't really scared, since Mary and the kids weren't there, but we were lucky nobody was hurt. The fire apparently had started when some people staying in the hotel for a convention of cleaners somehow got some different chemicals mixed up and there was an explosion. Our clothes smelled like smoke for a long time after that.

On the same trip, we went to New York, and after a game one day we came back to the hotel and found the entrances blocked by police officers who were not letting anyone enter. A robber had gone into the hotel, and the police were not letting anyone else in until the building was searched and he was captured.

Jack Buck always teases me about how careful I am in hotel rooms, making certain there is nobody hiding in the shower or in a closet or underneath a bed, and I guess I might be a little too cautious. I always put a chair underneath the door jam when I go to bed at night as well, making certain no one can enter the room.

In all the years I traveled as a player, coach and manager, I was only robbed once. When I was a coach for Whitey Herzog in the early 1980s, we were staying at the Grand Hyatt in New York. After we got back to the hotel following a game, Whitey asked all of the coaches to stop by his room for a drink and to discuss things. I went to my room first to put on a fresh shirt, and then went to Whitey's room.

I was gone for maybe an hour and a half, and when I got back to my room, there was something that didn't seem quite right. I always carry an alarm clock with me, and I noticed it wasn't where I had left it. My first thought was that the maid must have knocked it over when she came in to fix the bed, but I looked all over and couldn't find it.

Then I noticed my suitcase, and it looked as if it had been roughed up a little. The clothes hanging in the closet had been pushed around a bit, and then I figured out what had happened. I had been robbed.

Whoever had gotten into my room took a tie tack that was very special to me. They awarded players different items when they made the All-Star game when I played, like a cigarette box or a watch or this tie tack. It was from my fourth All-Star game, and it was crossed bats with a little diamond in it. It wasn't that expensive, but it was from the All-Star game and that meant a lot to me.

We had been in Montreal before coming to New York, and the robber had taken some perfume Mary had asked me to get for her and about $75 in Canadian money—and my $5 alarm clock.

What really ticked me off was when I called security to report the theft, the guy told me, "That's what we have safes for." I told the guy not even to come up to my room. I was only upset about the tie tack, because I couldn't replace it. It was a nice little gadget and I would have liked to have kept it.

I was telling the girls about Red being robbed and they said, "Mom, did they take any of his clothes?" I said, "Nobody would take those clothes that he wears." I wish they had so we could have gone and bought him some new ones. He will never be on the best dressed list. The most upsetting thing to me was that the perfume was stolen. I really wanted it.

— Mary Schoendienst

The team fell off to fourth-place finishes in 1969 and 1970, and even though we improved to second in 1971, we still were seven games behind the Pirates and not really in the race. A variety of moves were being discussed, and one I really wanted us to make was to trade for Joe Morgan, a young second baseman for the Astros.

I really thought we were going to get him, but then the Astros traded him to Cincinnati instead. Had we been able to make that deal, it really would have changed the course of the next several seasons.

One trade we did make, regrettably, was sending Steve Carlton to the Phillies during spring training in 1972. You could tell by watching Carlton pitch that he was going to be something special, and he already had won 20 games for us. He and Mr. Busch were in a contract dispute, however, and it got ugly and Mr. Busch ordered Bing to trade him and Bing got the best pitcher he thought he could find.

What's interesting about the trade was that at the time, nobody thought it was a terrible deal. Rick Wise had been a good pitcher, and nobody knew how good Carlton would become. It wasn't viewed then as it is today, perhaps the worst trade in Cardinals' history.

If we had kept Carlton and made the trade for Joe Morgan, there's no telling how many pennants we could have won in the 1970s. Even without either player, we came close twice, finishing 1 1/2 games out in both 1973 and 1974.

We did have good players on those teams. Gibson and Brock had become established as two of the best in the game and were headed for the Hall of Fame. Trading Cepeda to the Braves for Joe Torre had been a good deal.

Joe knew how to play, and he played hard. He was the type of player who you could tell was hoping to stay in the game after his playing career was over, and that was one of the reasons he paid close attention to what was going on, trying to soak up all of the knowledge that he could.

One of the pitchers on those teams in the early 1970s was veteran Moe Drabowsky, who was at the end of a long career. He used to play tricks with firecrackers, and I didn't like that because I was afraid somebody was going to get hurt. When I smelled the gunpowder one time, I made a blanket statement to the team that the next time somebody set off a firecracker, the entire team was going to be fined. That put an end to the fireworks.

All any manager can do is play the guys on his roster and hope for the best. When we had good players in 1967 and 1968, we won. In the 1970s, when there was a little dropoff in talent, we didn't win. Bing was a good GM and had a long run in the job, and he knew as well as I did that a couple of different moves might have meant we could have come out on top, but those moves were never made.

Being general manager might be the toughest job in baseball, because you truly are caught in the middle. On one side is the manager, arguing for the best players he can get, no matter the cost, and on the other side is the owner, telling him how much money he can spend. That balancing act is always difficult, even if you have the best manager in the world and the most generous owner with the deepest pockets. You also have to realize that even if you want to make a trade, your manager wants the deal and the owner says it's OK, you still have to get the other team to go along with it and sometimes that just doesn't happen.

It was fun to match wits with other managers like Walter Alston of the Dodgers. You could tell guys like Alston, Gene Mauch and Sparky Anderson knew what they were doing, and if they had good players, they were going to win. They let their guys play, and that's the way it should be. They also disciplined their players, letting them know who was boss.

Managers were not as big of celebrities in the 1970s as they are today, and certainly didn't command the kind of salaries the top managers pull in today. We did get some perks, however, and one came my way when I was asked to do a television commercial for Bow Wow dog food.

It was fun to do, but I didn't have a lot of other opportunities. Most of the people and companies that wanted me to do advertisements for them were interested in me wearing my uniform, which certainly would have made me more recognizable, but the Cardinals had the rights to anything using the uniform and they said no to the outside commercials. That was OK with me, because I never viewed myself as a star anyway.

I never really thought about how long I wanted to manage. I always was working on a one-year contract, so I never was able to look way down the road, but I enjoyed what I was doing, even when we weren't winning, and didn't think I was ready to do something else.

A writer in 1974 got a little carried away talking about me. Bill Christine wrote, "Schoendienst is one of those baseball oddities, a manager with a secure job. The day Schoendienst gets fired by the Cardinals, the Gateway Arch will keel into the Mississippi, Stan Musial will deny he's from Donora and Gussie Busch will endorse scotch."

He was wrong. None of those other things happened when after finishing third in 1975 and slipping to fifth in 1976, losing 90 games, I was fired.

It caught me a little off guard, as it would anybody, but I was proud of what I had accomplished. I managed the Cardinals for 12 seasons, the longest tenure for a manager in team history. At that time only five men had managed one club in the National League for more consecutive seasons—John McGraw, Walter Alston, Cap Anson, Wilbert Robinson and Fred Clarke.

The organization decided to make changes, it was as simple as that, and there really was no argument I could make. I never second-guessed myself, I never regretted any move or decision I made, and I was happy with the job I had done.

I was 53 years old, had been in baseball for 34 years and didn't know anything else. I didn't know what I was going to do, but I knew I would find a way to stay in baseball. I also wasn't willing to bet that someday I wouldn't be back with the Cardinals.

Chapter 10

HELLO, MR. FINLEY

There were some managerial jobs open after the 1976 season, including the Pirates, where Danny Murtaugh had retired. The job appealed to me because I thought they had a good ballclub, but they never called and instead hired Chuck Tanner, who had managed Oakland the previous year.

The A's didn't show any interest in me for the manager's job, hiring Jack McKeon, but we were sitting around the house on Thanksgiving when the telephone rang, and it was Charlie Finley.

Finley said he would like to hire me as one of his coaches, but first he had to talk to McKeon. He called back just a few minutes later and gave me McKeon's number and told me to call him, which I did.

We had a very pleasant conversation and McKeon and Finley hired me. I guess the order of those conversations should have told me all I needed to know about what it was going to be like working for an owner like Finley.

People say Gussie Busch was a very hands-on owner, getting involved in a lot of the decisions that he should have left to his baseball people. Compared to Finley, Gussie was a saint. Finley calling me about being a coach, instead of letting his new manager tell him who he wanted to hire as coaches was just one indication of the control he had on that ballclub.

I was thankful he had called, however, because now I had a job for the next season and didn't have to wonder anymore about what I was going to do.

Finley received a lot of criticism during his years owning the A's. He and commissioner Bowie Kuhn never saw eye-to-eye on matters. I liked Charlie, but I think he had a chip on his shoulder because Kuhn had overruled him and said he couldn't sell some of his best players, and he lost almost all of the players from his great teams in the early 1970s and didn't even get any prospects or money in return.

After the 1976 season, the A's lost Don Baylor, Rollie Fingers, Gene Tenace, Joe Rudi, Campy Campaneris and Sal Bando as free agents. About the only player they had left who had been on the World Champion teams was pitcher Vida Blue.

Even his famous mule, Charlie O., died that winter.

Before I left to join the A's in Arizona for spring training, the residents in my hometown of Germantown planned a big celebration to rename the town ballpark Schoendienst Field. It had been planned before I was fired by the Cardinals, and the people there went ahead with the plan and didn't change their minds. Everybody in my family came for the ceremony, including my mother, Mary. I threw out the first pitch and my son Kevin was the batter.

Musial was there and gave a speech, and former Cardinal announcer Buddy Blattner joked about how he and I had come up together as rookies and one scout predicted Blattner would become the better player.

"Ever since, that scout has been driving a bus in Syracuse," Blattner said.

One of the congratulatory telegrams I received was from my new boss, Finley.

"Congratulations to you, Red, for the honor of having a baseball field named after you. The best I have ever done was to have a mule named after me, Charlie O., who unfortunately passed away on December 17, 1976. I am now looking for a replacement for Charlie O. the mule, and this time the mascot will be a jackass—and

I assure you he will not be named Charlie O., but will be named after someone who, in my opinion, is a real jackass. I am sure your imagination is good enough to identify this person immediately. . . ."

Finley made no mentions of Kuhn in the telegram, so draw your own conclusions about who he was talking about. Later I heard one of the writers in Oakland saying something to Finley about Kuhn, noting that he was going on a trip to Japan. Quipped Finley, "I hope he's got a one-way ticket."

Dedicating the ballpark in my honor was a nice sendoff for spring training, and I was excited about joining a new ballclub and being in the American League for the first time. The only time I had seen any of the parks was for All-Star games and the World Series, and there were a lot of places I had never been. I was looking forward to returning to Boston, which had been one of my favorite cities when the Braves were still there.

I wasn't sure exactly what job McKeon had in mind for me, and as it turned out I did a little bit of everything. I worked with the infielders, spent time with the hitters and also coached either third base or first. Finley was trying to keep expenses low, so we didn't have all of the extra coaches teams have today and one of our coaches, Bobby Hofman, also doubled as the traveling secretary.

Nobody asked me if I had a favorite uniform number, and when I got to Arizona I found No. 43 hanging in my locker. I put it on and never said a word to anybody, because it didn't really bother me any. Mary came down later in the spring, and at a game one day, she ran into Finley. She was wearing her necklace with number 2 on it, and Finley asked about it and she told him that had been my number all of my years in St. Louis. Finley didn't say another word to Mary and never said anything about it to me, but the next day when I came to the ballpark my number had been switched to 2. He was good about a lot of things like that. He invited Mary to sing the National Anthem on opening day, and she did.

The only person I asked about Finley before agreeing to go to work for him was Dal Maxvill, my former player, who had been a coach for Oakland in 1975. He told me I would enjoy Finley, and he was right.

I can see where Finley could have intimidated a lot of people, and I never would have wanted to be his manager because of all the grief he put that person through, but as a coach we were pretty much immune from his criticism and trying to call us at all hours of the day and night. About the only time he looked for me, Hofman and Lee Stange, the pitching coach, was when he was in Oakland and wanted somebody to go with him to dinner.

Part of the reason he was like that, I think, was that he lived in Chicago and the team played in Oakland. He was involved with other businesses, and he never was in Oakland full time. He also was mad at Kuhn and blamed him for wrecking his team, and he knew he wasn't going to be competitive with the players he had, and he had not been able to get better prospects by trading off the good players he did have.

I didn't know how bad the team was going to be in 1977, and if I had known, I don't know if it would have changed my decision to take the job or not. We lost 98 games and finished last, 38 1/2 games out of first. McKeon didn't make it through the year, getting fired after 53 games and reassigned to the front office. Bobby Winkles took over, and he and I became good friends.

Winkles had a hard time putting up with Finley butting into his business. Finley used to love to call his manager in the dugout during the game. He would also call at 4 o'clock in the morning if he wanted to, it didn't matter to him that the team had not gotten in until 1 a.m. or so. He always had questions and he wanted explanations.

Winkles was a very good golfer, and I think part of the reason he liked to spend so much time on the course was so he wouldn't be interrupted by Finley calling him. This was in an era before cellular phones. Being on the course was his therapy, his stress relief. About three or four times a week, he would go out early in the morning, the first guy on the course, and take about four clubs in his bag. He would run around the course. He'd hit the ball, then run down the fairway, hit it again, and run to the green. He'd make his putt, then run to the next hole. He'd play the 18 holes in an hour or so. Of course he always was in the fairway so he didn't ever have to look for his ball.

One of the people who worked in the front office for Finley was a kid he had seen tap dancing and put him to work as a vice president or something—M.C. Hammer, who is now a famous rap star. I don't know exactly what Hammer was in charge of, but he was around all the time and I think was on the phone with Finley during most of the games telling him what was going on and whether the manager was doing the right thing or not.

Nobody was coming to the games. We drew less than 500,000 for the entire season, an average of about 6,800 a night. The largest crowd of the season was 32,000 to see the Yankees. It really wasn't surprising, however, because the A's weren't drawing even in the days they were winning, From their first season in Oakland, 1968, until 1980 they only drew 1 million fans or more twice, and then just barely over 1 million for a first-place team. It was no wonder Finley worried so much and was so upset—he had to be losing a lot of money.

Because we were doing so badly, Finley kept changing players. If anybody got hot in the minors for a few days, Finley rushed him to the big leagues. We always had guys walking in the clubhouse that we didn't know were coming until they showed up. Anybody who had a bad week was in danger of getting shipped out.

Finley had his brand of baseball that he wanted us to play, which was different than most of the American League teams. He wanted us to run, and he tried to get as many fast guys as possible on the team. He called them his rabbits.

We were playing the Twins in Minnesota one day and Finley came in from Chicago and had a meeting with the manager and coaches in the clubhouse before the game.

He had brought a kid up from A ball who supposedly was a good runner. At the meeting he told Winkles, "I want you to get a man on first base. I don't care if it's the fifth inning. Don't wait too long. I want the rabbit in there and I want him to run and steal a base."

Finley then looked at me. "Red," he said, "we're moving you over to first base because you stole a lot of bases in your day. You know how to run. I want you to tell these guys when to run and when not to run." Mike Marshall was pitching for the Twins, and

Charlie had held a grudge against him ever since the World Series a few years earlier, when he had been pitching for the Dodgers and had picked one of Finley's guys off first base. Finley said, "Marshall's got a good move." I said, "I know he has Charlie."

Finley had a rule that anybody who got picked off base was automatically fined, probably $50 or so. He really worried about those kinds of things.

We got into the sixth inning or so of the game, and got a guy on first. In came the kid to pinch-run. He was real nervous. I leaned over and told him, "Now this guy that's pitching is the guy we were talking about, Marshall. He's got a good move." The kid looked at me and said, "I can't get off too far or I'll get picked off. It's going to cost me money, and I don't make that much money."

The kid was telling me this while he was standing on first base. I couldn't believe it. I told him, "He may not give you his best move, but he's going to throw over here. Be careful." He said OK and stepped off the base about two steps. Here came Marshall's throw, and I'll be darned if he didn't pick the kid off, just like that.

Our next batter also got a hit. Finley also liked it when the runner tried to steal on the first two pitches, so he took off for second and was promptly thrown out. The next guy came up and also got a hit. He tried to steal second on the first pitch and he was thrown out. We had three hits in the inning and three guys thrown out.

Finley was sitting right behind the dugout, and as I got close to the dugout he yelled at me, "Nice coaching Red, Nice (expletive) coaching. I put my rabbit out there and you get him picked off." You could hear him all over the ballpark.

The score was tied in the ninth when we got a runner to third base. Hofman was coaching there. Finley also liked guys to tag up and try to score, and the batter hit a little popup right behind the shortstop. It was still in the infield. Bobby didn't send the guy, and the Twins got the next out and we didn't score. As he was coming into the dugout, Finley started yelling at him. He was hollering, "Nice coaching, Bobby. Where you got your hands? Get your hands out of your pockets and tell them when to go."

There never was a dull moment with Finley around, that's for sure.

Finley had nothing to do with the worst experience of the season, which came in September when we flying from Oakland to Kansas City. We were almost to Kansas City when we hit an awful electrical storm. It shook the plane a bunch of times. I really don't know how that plane stayed in the air. When those lightning bolts flashed, it was brighter than day. Everybody on the plane was scared to death. We had a pilot who had a lot of experience, and he said he was going to try to land in Kansas City, but he pulled back up and said it was too great a risk. We were lucky we had a pilot who knew what he was doing or we might have been in trouble.

We landed in Salina, Kansas, and took a bus to Kansas City. The next night we were at the ballpark, and it started raining so hard the water was coming up into the dugout and clubhouse. It was raining so hard you couldn't see the lights on the scoreboard in centerfield. That was the night Brush Creek flooded in the plaza area of Kansas City, killing a lot of people. It was the worst storm I ever saw.

When the umpires called the game, Winkles, Hofman and I were going to get a cab, but a friend of Hofman's was there with a car and he took us to the hotel. Some roads were blocked off. It was the first time in my life I actually saw water running uphill. That's how hard it was raining. I don't know how it could have been any worse.

With all of the trips I've taken over the years, I'm certain there were other close calls that we never knew anything about. The only other one I can recall was once with the Giants, when we were coming in to land, and there was a smokestack that looked like it was so close we could just reach out of the plane and touch it. We landed, and nobody ever said anything.

Finley wasn't happy about the way the season had gone, and I really thought there was a chance he was going to sell the team. One guy who wanted to buy it was Marvin Davis, who had made a lot of money in the oil business and owns about half of Colorado, I think. He wanted to move the team to Denver, where he lived.

Davis called me that winter, and he wanted me to fly into Denver to meet with him and tell him about the club. He was that sure he was going to buy it. I went, and we spent the day together and had lunch. He told me he would be looking for a manager and that I probably was going to be the guy.

All winter Davis kept thinking he was going to get the club, but it still hadn't happened by February, when it was time to report to Arizona for spring training. I had re-signed with Finley as a coach, since I didn't know for certain if anything was going to happen, and Winkles was coming back as the manager. We were playing a game against the Angels that spring, and I was coaching first base, when I heard someone shouting at me from the stands.

I turned around and it was Davis. After the inning ended, I went over to where he was standing, and he said, "I think I bought the club. I think we got it under control."

I talked with him after every inning, and he kept waiting, I guess for the attorneys or something, to get word to him about what was going on. He said he was leaving after the game, but he would be back in touch with me. I didn't hear from him for about a week, and then he called me.

"Red, this is getting ridiculous," he said. "I don't do business this way. Now he's got something else that he wants. I just want to let you know I'm calling it off. I'm not going to buy the club."

It had been so close that Davis even had real estate people in Denver sending us information about houses we could buy. He was a great guy, and he definitely wanted a team but it just didn't work out. If he had been able to buy the A's and move the team, the Colorado Rockies never would have come into existence. Instead, he bought a movie studio.

Not selling the team didn't seem to have any effect on Finley. He was just as involved and just as unpredictable as he had been the previous year.

We got off to a surprisingly good start, going 24-15, before Finley got in the way and messed things up. We had a day off, and the team was doing so well Winkles didn't schedule a workout or anything and told everybody to do what they wanted to do.

A group of us were going to play golf at a country club and have dinner, and Winkles left word with Finley that's where he was going to be. Somehow Finley didn't get the message, and he called

Winkles at 4 o'clock in the morning and really blasted him. "Where in the hell were you? You didn't leave word."

Winkles told him, "I told you, Charlie, we were going to be at the country club. I gave you the phone number and everything."

Finley said, "You're fired." Winkles shot back at him, "No I'm not fired, I quit."

I didn't know any of this until I got to the ballpark that day and Winkles told me he had quit. He was nervous and upset, but he just said he had had it with all of the phone calls and interference from Finley and being called all kinds of names. Winkles said, "I quit before he fired me."

Finley didn't really think Winkles was quitting. Winkles and I sat there in the clubhouse and talked, and about 30 minutes later the telephone rang. It was Finley; he wanted to talk to me. He said, "Will you sit down and talk with Bobby and tell him not to quit?" I told Finley we had been talking for 30 minutes. He said, "You tell him not to quit. I want him back as manager."

After I hung up, Bobby said there was no way he was coming back, I told him, "If you quit you won't get paid. If he fires you, he's got to pay you. He said, "I don't care."

A few minutes later the phone rang again. Finley was calling. "How'd you do?" he asked me. I told him Bobby was still going to quit. Then Finley said, "How about you?" "What about me?" I said.

He wanted to know if I would take over as manager. There was no way I was going to manage for him. I told Finley I'd like to stay on as a coach. He finally talked himself into bringing McKeon back out of the front office, and that's what he did. Winkles cleaned out his desk and left. I could have said, "Well, I'll take over, Charlie," and I would have been the new manager, but I didn't want the job.

After going back to coaching, I really didn't have much interest in becoming a manager again. A lot of guys will manage four or five teams and think nothing about it. They get fired at one place and simply move somewhere else. I thought 12 years as the manager of the Cardinals was long enough and I didn't want to be one of those guys who bounced around from city to city, job to job. Of course if I had known the money for managers was going to reach the levels it has now, I might have thought differently. The money wasn't there when I was playing, and it wasn't there when I was managing like it is now.

Finley had a lot of innovative ideas that I think probably were ahead of his time. He wanted to invent an orange baseball because he thought it would be easier to see. If he had been allowed to trade off his star players and get either money or prospects for them, I don't think he would have gotten so bitter and might have had better teams and remained in the game. He finally sold the A's in 1980 to the Wally Haas family, the head of the Levi Strauss Co., and the team got good again.

I called Finley from time to time, and he was really sick in the hospital when the Cardinals happened to be in Chicago. I called the hospital and asked to talk to him, but they said he wasn't talking with anybody or accepting any visitors. I told the nurse that I understood that, but that I had been one of his coaches and was in town and wanted to know if I could come by and see him or talk to him.

They called the room, and a nurse answered. I explained again who I was, and this time Finley took the call. "Come on up, Red," he said. When I got to his room the nurse said, "You can't stay too long." I must have been there for two hours, and we had a really nice visit. He kept telling me not to leave, to stay and talk a while. He really enjoyed it.

He asked when the club was leaving, and he said the next time I was in Chicago he would show me some good places to eat. I talked to him a few more times after that, but I never saw him again before he died. He was different, but I enjoyed being with him. You had to stay on your toes, because he had something going on all the time.

I never regretted telling Finley I didn't want to manage his club. That team didn't have much talent, and we quickly sank toward the bottom of the division again. We lost 93 games, only this time we finished sixth instead of last.

Despite the struggles on the field, I enjoyed seeing the different stadiums and watching some of the great players in the American League that I hadn't seen play before. I wish some of them had been on our team, but that wasn't the case.

Our best player probably was Mitchell Page, an outfielder who was a good baserunner, Finley's kind of player. Had he been surrounded by a better supporting cast, he could have been an even better player. Instead, we kept bringing in young guys who weren't ready and trying to make the best of the situation.

We were in Baltimore one day in 1978, and Finley was there and said, "Red, I want you to come with me. I just signed up a young kid and I want you to watch him throw." We walked across the field at Memorial Stadium to where the kid was warming up. He popped the ball good, and I thought he looked like a good prospect. Finley and I watched for a few minutes, then walked back across the field, and Finley asked me what I thought.

"He's got a good live arm," I said. "It looks like he might be a pretty good pitcher. Don't rush him along; let him develop in Class A or Double A and let him get some experience and then he can progress and move up."

Finley stopped me and said, "Red that's where you're wrong. He's pitching Thursday, right here."

The kid was Mike Morgan. The A's had picked him in the first round of the draft, and a week after graduating from high school with no professional experience, he made his debut against the Orioles. He actually pitched OK, losing 3-0, but pitching a complete game. He started two more games, and lost them both, before Finley sent him to Triple A for the rest of the season.

Years later Morgan ended up with the Cardinals, and we talked about that game. Finley was wrong to do that, and he did it with other guys besides Morgan. He was taking a real chance that he wasn't going to screw up their careers, all for the personal satisfaction of seeing the guy start off in the majors. He didn't even do it as a promotional stunt to hype the attendance, because we were on the road. That's when somebody needed to be in a position to tell Finley he couldn't do that, but there was nobody there with that authority.

Other than not having a good ballclub, the worst part about coaching in Oakland was that it was so far away from St. Louis. The girls and Kevin were growing up and were involved in a lot of activities, so it was not realistic to expect them to pick up and move. I never intended to move our home away from St. Louis anyway, so Mary and the kids stayed in St. Louis most of the time those two summers. Mary and Kevin did come to Kansas City and sometimes when the A's were in Chicago, so we did get together as much as we could.

When you look at the big picture, I realize what I went through those two years being separated so much from Mary and the kids is what a lot of players, coaches and managers go through every season. I knew I was lucky to have played so long and managed so long in one place, where I made my home, so I could be there when Mary and the kids needed me and for all of the big events in their lives.

When I got fired by the Cardinals after the 1976 season, I said the day might come where I could come back to St. Louis and that chance came in the winter of 1978. Ken Boyer, my former third baseman, had replaced Vern Rapp as manager early in the year and was looking to make some changes on his coaching staff. He wanted to know if I would like to be his hitting coach. It wasn't a tough decision.

Boyer had been a great player for the Cardinals, and he's one guy who deserved more consideration for the Hall of Fame. He was a consistent player, and he knew the game. He seemed to me to be the kind of guy who would do well as a manager, and he might have succeeded had been given a little more talented players.

Kenny inherited a bad team, and a team that was in a great deal of upheaval because Rapp had tried to be a tough disciplinarian, only to see it cause a player revolt, led by Ted Simmons. Kenny was a much more relaxed, player-oriented kind of manager, but he was just caught in the wrong place at the wrong time. We won 86 games in 1979, finishing 10 games over .500, but that wasn't the type of season Busch wanted. He had gone a long time without winning—more than a decade—and he was getting restless.

Devine had gotten fired again, and was replaced by John Claiborne, a young guy who Busch thought was ready to be the general manager. When the team started slowly in 1980, Busch decided he couldn't wait any longer to make a move.

Whitey Herzog, a native of New Athens, Illinois, had been fired by the Royals at the end of the 1979 season. He had been very successful in Kansas City, and Busch decided he wanted him to become the new manager.

On June 8, Claiborne flew to Montreal and because he didn't get there until after the first game had begun, he waited until in between games to fire Boyer. Later that day, the new manager—Whitey Herzog —was introduced to the media in a news conference at Busch's home at Grant's Farm.

A new era in Cardinals' history was on the horizon.

Chapter 11

WHITEYBALL

ermantown and New Athens are only about a half-hour apart as the crow flies, but I am eight years older than Whitey, so I already was with the Cardinals when he starting playing ball around the area.

I knew of Whitey, of course, and he knew of me, and we had a couple of occasions to get together before he came to work for the Cardinals.

One time I stayed at his house in Kansas City when I was there for a function, and another time when he was managing the Royals and I was with Oakland, he took me dove hunting. Mary and I also went to a dinner in New Athens when he was being honored by a group there, but we really had not spent much time together and didn't know each other well.

While I was sorry to see Boyer get fired, I thought the Cardinals made a good choice in bringing in Whitey. He had been a good manager in Kansas City but got fired when he and the owner's wife couldn't agree on things, and those battles never come out in favor of the manager. Whitey had done everything there was to do in the game—player, coach, manager, scout, minor league coordinator—so I knew he had an idea what he was doing and would be a very good judge of a player's ability.

One thing nobody would have been able to predict on that June afternoon when he and Gussie sat next to each other at the news conference was how close the two of them would become in a very short amount of time.

Whitey spoke Gussie's language—brash, direct, never afraid to ruffle any feathers. I don't think Whitey has ever been scared or afraid or been in awe of anyone or anything in his life. He didn't care if Gussie didn't like what he had to say. If Gussie got mad and fired him, Whitey would have gone back to the lake and fished or played golf until somebody else needed a manager and called him.

Gussie loved that kind of style, however. He went toe-to-toe with Whitey and quickly gave him all the power and control he needed to break up the Cardinals and put the team back together again. That meant making Whitey the general manager in addition to being the manager, replacing Claiborne.

In addition to being a great evaluator of talent, Whitey knew how to handle people. He knew he could be direct and argumenta-tive with Gussie, but around other people he had to speak more quietly and be more complimentary than harsh. He was very much in control of himself, and it didn't take long before he got control of the team and the organization.

Whitey had only been managing a few weeks when he knew he had undertaken a bigger task and assignment than he had first realized. We had three of the highest paid players in the game in Keith Hernandez, Ted Simmons and Garry Templeton, all extremely talented, but Whitey didn't like the mix on the ballclub. He wanted a team that relied more on speed and defense, with good relief pitch-ers, and he didn't think the Cardinals had that.

When he told Gussie he didn't think the team he had taken over was ever going to win, Gussie gave him permission to make the moves he wanted to make. One reason I think Whitey said OK to being the general manager even though he didn't really want the job was that he knew it was the one way to insure that he did get the players and types of players that he wanted on his club.

What Whitey didn't have was knowledge of the players in the Cardinals' farm system, and he thought he needed to know what help was coming from that area before he could think of making possible moves. In order to check out those players on his own, he decided to turn over the managing duties to me for the rest of the season, freeing him up to go watch the minor leaguers as well as other teams.

Whitey told me to run the club the way I wanted, but I knew one thing he was interested in was finding out if we had any young guys who could play. I called him one night and said I'd like to play this kid, Tommy Herr, at shortstop if it was all right with Whitey. I told Whitey I knew he was not a shortstop and was a second baseman, but this way I could get him some playing time and see what he could do. Whitey was all in favor of the idea.

I told Tommy the next day about my plan. I told him, "I know you're not a shortstop, but this will give you some playing time." He said that was OK with him, and he went out and played hard and did a good job. The next year he was our second baseman, and one piece of the puzzle was in place.

At the winter meetings in Dallas that year, Whitey made two big trades that expedited the rebuilding process. In an 11-player deal with San Diego, he acquired Rollie Fingers. A day later, he swung a deal with the Cubs, acquiring Bruce Sutter in exchange for Leon Durham and Ken Reitz. The Cubs had wanted Herr instead of Reitz, but Whitey had been adamant that he wouldn't trade Tommy.

In two days, we had gone from no relievers to having two of the best in the game. Whitey was willing to see if he could make the combination work, until he found out that Simmons was balking at Herzog's plan to move him to first base and shift Hernandez to left field. Whitey set out to see if he could trade Simmons, and he did, along with Fingers, to Milwaukee.

In a week's time, Whitey had traded away 13 players and added nine, including his old catcher from Kansas City, Darrell Porter, who signed as a free agent.

One of the things Whitey did in making all of those moves was improve the character of the team. Whitey was a disciplinarian, but he had simple rules. He wanted guys to be at the ballpark on time, to hustle, not to miss signs, and that was about it. He never tried to control guys away from the ballpark or tell them what they could or couldn't do—a manager could go crazy if he tries to run everybody's business all the time. If you did what he asked when you were in uniform, Whitey didn't really worry about the rest of your day.

Whitey had been in the game long enough to know that being a manager wasn't exactly brain surgery. There were certain points in a game when decisions had to be made, but managing a club was kind of like cooking a steak. If you have good enough players, you won't be able to screw it up too easily. If you have a good enough piece of meat, you can hardly ruin the thing unless you burn it up.

Where Whitey stood out from other managers was in his ability to predict moves in advance. He always knew if he made a pitching change what response the other team was going to make. He was able to anticipate matchups as far as a couple of innings in advance, and that let him always have his guys prepared and get the matchup that he wanted. He made the best use of his players possible, and even though he liked to use a regular lineup, he knew enough to keep the extra guys fresh and make certain they felt part of the team because he knew he was going to need them in order to be successful. He had been a utility player himself, and he knew they had feelings and emotions as well and didn't like feeling they weren't appreciated or part of the club. That was where all of Whitey's people skills really worked to his advantage.

Whitey liked all of the moves he had made, and he thought the Cardinals who reported to St. Petersburg in 1981 had a much better chance of winning than the team from the previous year. We might have won, too, had the season not been interrupted by a strike by the players that lasted almost two months.

I've said before that I don't think anything good ever comes out of a strike, and this was another example of that. It was just a sign of the growing escalation of the split between the players and the owners that was only going to increase over the years. If the owners had been able to make peace with the players at that point it might have prevented a lot of the problems that developed later.

All of the coaches were still getting paid during the strike, so the Cardinals had to find jobs for us to do. Most of us went to work with some of the minor league teams, and that meant one lucky assignment for me—I got to go to the Quad Cities for a few days, where my son Kevin was playing for the Cubs' farm team.

I never pushed Kevin into playing baseball, but he was around it all his life so it was natural he picked it up. It looked like he had a lot of possibilities when he was young, in his early teens, because it looked like he knew how to play. He sprained his thumb when he was in high school, however, and he kept getting hurt. He just couldn't stay healthy.

He was an infielder, playing second, short and third, and after high school he played at Meramec Community College. He played one game in which his cousin, Chris, was pitching a no-hitter against Meramec. Kevin came up in the ninth and broke it up with a double. I don't know if they ever talked about it. Kevin got a chance to sign with the Cubs—his mother was his agent—and I know he's glad he played for a couple of years even though he never got above A ball. He decided on his own he probably wasn't going to go much further so he had better start doing something else. Mary was glad he played, but she also was glad when he stopped. It was harder and made her more nervous to watch him play than it had been for her to watch me.

The girls all liked baseball as well. Cathleen and Colleen were great softball players. Cathy was a real instinctive player; wherever the ball was she was going to be at the same spot. She could run too. All the girls loved the game and still do. They don't want me to quit or retire because they still want to go to the game once in a while.

Eileen's favorite player was Harmon Killebrew of the Twins. She was hung up on him, and I don't know how she picked him. It must have been in the World Series or All-Star game or something. He was her favorite player, and every time Red was someplace where they would be together she wanted Red to get his autograph. "Tell him he's the best player going," she used to say, and she was sincere about it.

When we went to Cooperstown with Red, Harmon was there and Red introduced Eileen to him. He was very gracious talking with her.

— Mary Schoendienst

My kids, and other kids who grew up during the same generation, had a harder time following baseball than did people in my generation. When I was a kid, if you picked out a favorite player and became a fan, you knew he was going to be on the ballclub and never had to worry about it. That started to change when my kids were growing up, and today it's almost impossible for kids to know where players are going to be. As soon as they become free agents, most of them just pick up and go to whatever team is willing to pay them the most money. It makes it very hard to follow players and teams, with so many changes taking place all the time. I still have people come up to me and tell me I was their favorite player and it's a nice thing to hear. I don't think kids today will ever be able to say that, because their favorite player changes almost every year.

Whitey wasn't done making changes to the Cardinals despite all of his moves the year before. He traded an OK pitcher, Bob Sykes, to the Yankees for a minor-league outfielder, Willie McGee, and dealt pitchers Silvio Martinez and Larry Sorensen to the Indians for outfielder Lonnie Smith. That left just one problem spot on the team—shortstop.

Garry Templeton had a lot of talent but he also had a lot of problems. After he had an embarrassing incident at Busch Stadium where he made some obscene gestures to the crowd, Whitey knew he had to get rid of him. He also had to get a shortstop to replace Templeton in the deal, however, and there really were only two guys who he thought fit what he was looking for—Ivan DeJesus of the Cubs and a youngster out in San Diego, Ozzie Smith.

When I was with Oakland and we trained in Arizona, I saw Ozzie play for San Diego quite a bit. I liked the way he played and the way he went about his business. He seemed to take directions real well and follow instructions, and while you knew he was never going to be a power hitter, not many shortstops are. Based on the input and suggestions of all of his staff, Whitey decided to try to trade Templeton for Smith and he was finally able to pull off the deal.

Whitey always was very good about seeking advice and opinions of everybody he knew and trusted before he made any decisions. He knew he was going to be the one held accountable if the deal was good or bad, but he wanted that decision to be based on as much information as possible. He listened to his coaches and respected his coaches and the other people who worked for him, and he knew we were all working for the same goal, trying to build a winning team.

He had taken some major—and unpopular—risks, trading away fan favorites like Simmons and a future Hall of Famer in Fingers. His attitude never wavered, however, and when anybody criticized him, he always had the same comeback—you haven't won in a dozen years anyway, why not let me try it my way.

In 1982, Whitey's way turned out to be the winning way. All of his moves had done exactly what Whitey had tried to do, give us a team with more speed and that played better defense so we could take advantage of the dimensions of our own stadium. With Lonnie Smith as the catalyst, we put runners on the bases, generated a lot of excitement and got enough pitching that we were able to run.

The media even coined the phrase "Whiteyball" for the style of play—getting a guy on first, stealing second, moving to third on a groundout and scoring on a fly ball. It was simple, fundamental baseball and it worked. We won the Eastern Division by three games over the Phillies, swept the Braves in the playoffs and faced Milwaukee— Simmons' new team—in the World Series.

The final piece of Whitey's puzzle had been assembled in May, when McGee came up from Louisville to play center field in place of the injured David Green. He wasn't supposed to stay more than a few weeks, but those plans quickly changed.

Green was an interesting, but sad, story. He was one of the players Whitey brought in from Milwaukee in the Simmons' trade and he had a great deal of talent. He was as good a young prospect as you cared to see, but he was from Nicaragua and had a lot of personal problems. He didn't discipline himself too well and got himself into trouble.

He could have been a great player, but he couldn't get over those personal problems. He did hit 15 homers for us in 1984, but that was just another glimpse of how good a player he could have been had he not gotten himself into so much trouble off the field.

A lot of times you see young prospects who look like they are going to become great players but they never make it. One reason is because they are afraid to do a little extra for themselves. They reach a certain level and they are afraid to go any higher. They are afraid to try a little harder to reach a little farther, because then somebody might expect them to do that every year. They think about things like that rather than just going out and playing and letting their natural talent and ability take over. I don't know if they get scared or what, but it's a shame when guys waste the kind of talent that a David Green had.

Most of the guys on that 1982 team were the kinds of players Whitey liked because they didn't waste anything. They busted their rears to play 100 percent all of the time and did the little things extra that meant the difference between winning and losing. The common theme of players who are on a winning team is they have the desire to win and they know how to win. A lot of players play in the major leagues for a long time without ever making it to the World Series, and sometimes there's a reason for that. They may be great players, but for some reason they don't know how to win.

When Whitey made all of his moves rebuilding the team, he looked for guys who had won before or knew how to win. Hernandez was already here, but he was that kind of player. About the only thing he didn't do well on the field was run, but you can't have everything. He was an outstanding defensive first baseman, and he had good knowledge of what he could do and what he wanted to do. He wasn't a great pull hitter, but he did a good job of hitting the ball from the second baseman over to left field.

He always impressed me the way he played in the field even if he went through a hitting slump. A lot of guys will take their batting problems into the field with them, lose their concentration, and mess up defensively as well. Even if Keith went 0-for-4, he might come up with a play in the field that would help the team win. That's the kind of concentration it takes to be a good player.

Tommy Herr was just a solid player. We got him back to his natural position of second base and everything fell into place for him. He was like Hernandez in the sense that he knew what he could do well and he didn't try to do something he wasn't capable of doing. There were a lot of players who might have had more talent than Herr, but they didn't know how to win the way he did. He was always in the game and always on top of things.

All of the expectations for Ozzie Smith were that he would play great defensively but would struggle with the bat. What nobody could tell in watching him play in San Diego, however, was how good a player he would become when he went to a good club.

Ozzie worked hard at becoming a good player and he made himself stronger and became a better offensive player. He knew he wasn't going to go out and hit a lot of homers, but he knew he could get hits, run well and steal a base, and make himself a complete player. That's exactly what he did.

Ken Oberkfell moved to third base to replace Reitz and make room for Herr at second. He was a tough player and did little things necessary to help the team win. He was from the St. Louis area, Maryville, Illinois, and I remember when the scouts brought him in to work out at Busch Stadium before we signed him. I liked his makeup then, and I wasn't surprised that he turned out to be a good major league player.

Lonnie Smith was another guy who seemed to win no matter where he went in his career, and I don't think that's merely a coincidence. He has a lot of desire, and he played the game hard. He could break up a double play as well as anybody. He wasn't that great an outfielder and he didn't have a tremendous arm, but when the game was on the line he always seemed to make the play or the throw that needed to be made. He was another guy who messed himself up, and if that hadn't happened I think he would have been able to play a little longer and have a little more success.

When Willie McGee came up he was a shy kid, and in many respects, he's the same today as he was 15 years ago. He was always listening, always asking questions, wanting to learn anything he could to become a better player. He went out and worked hard every day on all facets of the game—hitting, defense, baserunning. He likes to play, he likes the game, and that's refreshing. Everything he does on the field, he does hard.

Our rightfielder was George Hendrick, and he was the kind of player who gave you 100 percent all of the time when he was on the field, but then he wanted to get away from the park as quickly as possible, He didn't talk to reporters, preferring to leave that duty to the manager and other players, and he was happy if he could just do his job and be left alone.

Darrell Porter had a lot of critics because it was his misfortune to replace the popular Simmons, but he was a good player for the Cardinals. He was a strong guy, and since Whitey had known him so well he knew exactly what kind of player he would be. He always seemed to do a little extra at a crucial moment, like in the World Series.

His opposite-field hit in the second game of the series kept us from falling behind, two games to none. McGee became a national hero in game three in Milwaukee, and a rookie pitcher, John Stuper, came up big in game six to force a deciding game seven. A two-run single by Hernandez and an RBI single by Hendrick put us ahead to stay, and when Sutter struck out Gorman Thomas in the ninth, the Cardinals were once again World Champions.

I was a coach, not a player or the manager, but there is still no greater thrill than being in the locker room of a World Series champion. It's what you work for all year, and only one team gets to enjoy that feeling of tremendous release. We had a great parade through downtown St. Louis, and Whitey or McGee or any of the other guys could have run for Mayor and won in a landslide.

I enjoyed being a coach, because I believed I was able to make some contributions and I still was able to be around the game that I love. Whitey made it easy for his coaches to feel involved, because he was always asking for our opinions and suggestions and wanting to talk about the game.

One thing we didn't have on that 1982 team was a lot of power. We won with speed and defense and a lot of good contact hitters. Probably our best hitter was Keith Hernandez. Like Simmons and others before him, he was extremely popular and a fan favorite—but Whitey didn't let that interfere when he made the decision to trade Hernandez to the Mets in 1983. Hernandez was going to be a free agent at the end of the season, and Whitey didn't think the Cardinals were going to be able to sign him. There may have been other reasons behind the deal for Neil Allen—it turned out to be a horrible trade—but the bottom line is that we had to replace Hernandez at first base and we really spent a couple of years trying to find that player before swinging a trade with the Giants to acquire Jack Clark before the 1985 season.

Even if the goal of your team is speed and defense, you have to have a guy who is capable of hitting home runs. It may not be "sit on your heels and wait for a three-run homer" kind of offense, but still your lineup needs to have a power threat in it, and the Cardinals finally got that with Clark.

Clark didn't hit for a great average, but he got a lot of big hits and he did bomb some important home runs. He wasn't the only addition that helped put the team back in the playoffs again after a two-year absence.

Two other key players came out of the farm system, outfielder Vince Coleman and third baseman Terry Pendleton. Coleman stepped in to replace Lonnie Smith, and Pendleton took over for Oberkfell and both quickly made good impressions.

Coleman was our leadoff hitter and catalyst. I don't think many people expected him to be as good a player as he became, despite his speed. He was kind of like McGee three years earlier when he came up and never went back to the minors. Coleman was called up under similar circumstances and ended up being the NL Rookie of the Year.

The only problem Vince had was he and his agent made a bad decision when he decided to take an offer from the Mets a few years later and leave as a free agent. He had almost as good an offer from the Cardinals and had he stayed, he would have remained almost as popular a player as McGee.

Pendleton was another winning-type player. He knew what he had to do to help the team win, and he was a very steady player. All of those young guys like McGee, Coleman and Pendleton kind of came under the care and guidance of Ozzie Smith, even on an unofficial basis, and I think they learned a lot about the game and about life from him. They were good players and they were good people, too.

Our pitching staff had changed as well, but we still had Bob Forsch and Joaquin Andujar. Andujar and Tudor each won 21 games that year, and Forsch was still a very steady veteran. Bob is just a first-class guy on and off the field, and he gave you everything he had, every time he went to the mound. He pitched two no-hitters in his career, but perhaps the best thing about him was that he definitely was a team-oriented player. He didn't care at all about his personal performance as long as the team won.

Andujar was an interesting guy to have on the team, because you never knew what he was going to do. He had a lot of ability, and he also had a lot of confidence in our pitching coach, Hub Kittle, who also had coached Joaquin in Houston, and in Whitey. Both of those guys kind of got into Joaquin's head a little and gave him some confidence that he could be a good pitcher.

We won the division title, then beat the Dodgers in the playoffs on the strength of a couple of home runs, one by Ozzie in game five and the other by Clark in game six. It was a happy group of coaches and players who prepared to play Kansas City in the World Series.

Whitey never said so publicly, but I really think he wanted to win that series as kind of a personal proving ground. He had been fired by the Royals, and even though he had won the world championship in 1982, he still had some bad feelings about some of the people in the Kansas City organization.

The Royals had a good team, and they had a lot of great young pitchers. You could tell they had confidence in what they were doing, it was a nice matchup, and it really wasn't a surprise that the series ended up going seven games.

We really should have won the series in six games, however, if not for a missed call by umpire Don Denkinger at first base in the ninth inning. It was one of those plays that has been analyzed, discussed and criticized forever, and it probably will never end. My take on it was that he missed the call, but those things happen. It just so happens that when you miss them in the World Series, or make an error in the series, it becomes much more magnified because the whole country is watching. I know he didn't miss the call on purpose, and he felt bad about it and later said he blew it, but that didn't change the result.

As professionals, we should have been able to block that call out of our minds and concentrate on preparing for game seven the next night but that didn't happen. We should have had just as good a chance to win that game as the Royals, with Tudor pitching against young Bret Saberhagen, but we didn't. We fell behind early and ended up getting blown out, 11-0. Whitey and Andujar both got kicked out of the game by Denkinger, working the plate, and it wasn't a pretty sight.

Andujar was traded to Oakland over the winter—probably on orders from the brewery—and we had another bad season in 1986. Most of our regular lineup remained intact, however, and we rose back to the top in 1987 to win the division, beat the Giants in the playoffs and face Minnesota in the World Series.

The unfortunate luck of the draw had given the American League team the home-field advantage in the series, and this year it definitely wasn't an advantage. I've got nothing against domed stadiums, and in some climates they are definitely necessary. Miami needs one that they don't have, and if they get it, they will draw better and might be an even better team than the one that won the 1997 World Series.

I don't think Minnesota really needs a dome, and if they do, they need a better one than the one they've got. I've never been in a stadium where it was so hard to pick up the ball, and the only reason the Twins could do it was because they had played so many games there. Our guys didn't have a chance.

We won all three games at home, but they won the first three at their place to once again force game seven. In all nine World Series I have been involved in as a player, manager or coach, all of them went seven games. It was just meant to be that way, I guess.

Game seven of a World Series is as dramatic as you can get in a baseball season, and it creates the most nerves for the players. You always say you don't get nervous as a player, but that's not entirely accurate. I do know you get more nervous when you don't play, because there is nothing you can do that will affect the outcome of the game. Playing gets rid of some of the nervousness.

We lost again, this time by a score of 4-2, and the most disappointed players in our clubhouse were Clark and Pendleton. Clark had not been able to play because of torn ligaments in his ankle, and Pendleton was out with a rib-cage injury. If either had been able to play, it might have made the difference, but we'll never know.

Whitey has always said that he believes winning those pennants in 1985 and 1987 gave Gussie Busch something to live for. Gussie got a thrill out of riding his Clydesdale beer wagon around the field before the World Series, and those were among the happiest days of his life.

When Whitey was hired, he promised Gussie he would get him another world championship and more pennants and he had delivered. Gussie was falling into poor health, but whenever I would see him, he'd say, "A pleasure to see you, my man." Gussie was a great guy, and he loved baseball. I don't know if when he bought the team in 1953 he thought he would grow to love it as much as he did, but I agree with Whitey that it made the last years of his life some of the happiest ones.

When Gussie died on September 29, 1989, the almost universal opinion was that things were about to change for the organization. Gussie's death probably meant more to Whitey than to anybody else in the organization. Even when Gussie was not totally in control of what was going on, Whitey still was able to go to him and get his blessing for whatever moves he wanted to make. Dal Maxvill had taken over for Whitey's pal, Joe McDonald, as general manager, but Whitey's relationship with Gussie still was the key to getting things done.

After Gussie died, the executives at Anheuser-Busch got involved in baseball decisions, especially when they called for spending money, and Whitey quickly became very frustrated. There were things he wanted to do, and moves he wanted to make, and he kept getting blocked.

There were 10 players who were in the final year of their contracts in 1990, and Whitey wanted some decisions made to clear up their status. He thought the players were thinking too much about their own futures instead of the united goal of trying to help the team win. No matter how many times he brought up the subject, however, nothing changed and no decisions were made.

The team was playing poorly, with a record of 33-47, and we were in last place in the NL East. We were in San Francisco and had a terrible series before moving down the coast to San Diego. Everybody around him knew that Whitey was upset, but he didn't let anybody know he was thinking of taking some dramatic action.

Mike Shannon had a good friend who lived in San Diego, and he invited Whitey and the coaches to his house for dinner. While we were there, Whitey came up to me and said, "I want to see you when we leave here. When you leave I want to go back with you."

Looking back on it, I wonder if he was going to tell me what was going on. When we jumped in the same car to go back to the hotel, however, there were other people with us. He wanted me to come up to his room, but there were other people around and we couldn't get off by ourselves. We just forgot about it.

When I went into my room, I found a note that had been slipped under the door from Brian Bartow, our public relations director. He knew I had planned to leave early in the morning to play golf with Shannon. The note said, "Don't leave tomorrow. Stay here. Don't go anywhere."

I called Bartow and asked him what was going on. He said he didn't know, but that he had been told by Fred Kuhlmann and some of the other team executives to leave me the note that I needed to stay put through the next morning. I went to bed wondering what was going on.

We all found out the next day. Whitey surprised everybody by resigning. I got a call to meet with Kuhlmann and Maxvill at their hotel, and they said "changes are being made and Whitey is leaving." They wanted me to take over as the interim manager until they could hire somebody.

I was shocked, but it just showed Whitey was more upset than he had been letting on. I've never asked Whitey about it since, and he's never talked about it with me. He went to work for the Angels as general manager for a couple of years, but has never managed again. The changing attitude of the players really got to him, in addition to the indifferent attitude he faced in his own front office.

It probably would have upset me too if I had been the full-time manager. I had received some overtures about managing again when

I was with Oakland, from people other than Marvin Davis, and when I got back to St. Louis, but I deflected the interest. I said I had had my run, and was happy doing what I was doing.

I told Kuhlmann and Maxvill I was there to do whatever they wanted, and would run the team until the new manager was hired. They said it would be about 10 days, but it was closer to three weeks. The favorite candidate from the minute Whitey quit was another former player of mine, Joe Torre, who had managed the Mets and Braves and at the time was working as a broadcaster for the Angels. He and Maxvill were big buddies, and that's who Dal wanted and got for the job.

Torre had been a good player for me and was a guy I thought would make a good manager. I was glad the new boss was a fan favorite of the Cardinals because that made the transition after Whitey a little easier than it otherwise might have been. It also allowed me to keep my job.

While all of the Cardinals' success in the 1980s had been great, my personal highlight came on a sunny July afternoon in 1989 in Cooperstown, N.Y., when I became a member of baseball's Hall of Fame.

Chapter 12

THE HALL OF FAME

Anyway you look at it, it's hard to get to Cooperstown, N.Y.

Visitors to the tiny New York village have to drive through the winding routes in the state's countryside to get to baseball's hallowed shrine, the Hall of Fame.

For players and others in the game trying to get there to earn the ultimate recognition for their career, the path is even tougher. That's the way it should be, however. There shouldn't be anything easy about making the Hall of Fame.

Fans watching today's players often make statements such as, "That guy's a Hall of Famer," but I don't think they should make that judgment so quickly and easily. It takes more than just physical ability to make the Hall of Fame, and that's the way it should be, too.

The rules do a good job of controlling the election procedures to keep any questionable players out of the Hall. There are two ways a player can earn election, being voted in by the writers or selected by the Veteran's Committee.

After a player's career is completed, he must wait five years before he can be placed on the ballot for election by the writers. Only in very special cases—such as when the great Roberto Clemente was killed in a plane crash—is the five-year wait waived.

This is a good rule because it forces a writer to go back and look at a player's career before he votes, rather than just going on memory, and maybe a little sentiment, and voting for him the year after he retires.

Before a player's name goes on the Hall of Fame ballot, he has to pass through a screening committee. This committee does a good job of eliminating those players whose credentials don't merit Hall of Fame consideration but would clutter up the ballot if the names of everybody who was eligible was listed on the ballot.

In order to vote for the Hall of Fame, a writer must have been an active member of the Baseball Writers Association of America for more than 10 years. This is also a good rule—it means guys who pass through baseball but don't make a career out of covering the game and writing about it can't vote. There are always some exceptions, guys who earned a card without really ever covering very many games, but not enough that it makes much of a difference.

To be elected, a player must be named on at least 75 percent of the ballots that are cast. No player has ever received 100 percent and been elected unanimously. That's wrong. There are some great players, like Musial and Ted Williams, who should have been named on every ballot. There's no way a writer can justify not voting for a guy like that, but there are writers who purposely won't vote for a player because they don't want anybody to ever get 100 percent of the votes.

A player who is not elected can remain on the ballot for 15 years if he receives 5 percent or more of the vote. This is a rule that just went into effect a few years ago, and it has kept some pretty good players from remaining on the ballot and possibly receiving more votes. If a player doesn't receive the minimum vote of 5 percent, it also means he cannot later be considered by the Veterans Committee.

If a player doesn't get elected within his 15 years of eligibility by the writers, he has to wait another five years and then he can be considered by the Veteran's Committee, a group of former players, writers, broadcasters and executives. This committee's job also is to elect managers, umpires and executives to the Hall of Fame. It's never an easy task, because there always are more worthy candidates than can be selected by either the writers or the Veterans Committee.

I never thought about making the Hall of Fame when I played, I honestly didn't. Some players will say that, but they are as full of holes as Swiss cheese. I said I never thought about becoming a manager when I played either, and that's also true. Thinking like that might have messed me up.

My attitude always was that it would be great if I made it, but I wasn't going to lose any sleep if I didn't make it. I probably thought about it a little more in 1969, when Musial went in, and I hoped I would join him someday, but I really didn't know what was going to happen.

I didn't get to go to Stan's induction because I was managing the Cardinals. Mary was invited and went and had a nice time. I had been to Cooperstown twice for the Hall of Fame game, an exhibition played at Doubleday Field between an NL and AL team the day after the induction ceremony. On those trips, we flew in to Syracuse and bused to Cooperstown, getting there just in time to play the game and leaving immediately after, so there never was any time to take a tour and see what the place was really like.

During the years I was on the ballot for consideration by the writers, I never knew if I was going to be elected or not, but I never waited around to find out. I made certain I was always hunting or something that day so I wouldn't sit around the house all day waiting for a telephone call that might never come.

As it turned out, I wasn't elected by the writers. The closest I came was in 1981, when I received 166 votes. After the second five-year wait, I became eligible for consideration by the Veterans Committee when it met in Tampa in March of 1989.

Mary and I were in St. Petersburg with the Cardinals, and this time I decided to wait around the condo and see if the telephone rang. The 17 members of the committee who were present deliberated for nearly five hours before Ed Stack of the Hall of Fame called and told me I had been elected along with Al Barlick, the former umpire.

Mary had planned to go shopping, but she stayed home as well so she also was there when the call came.

Everybody was very excited and we were jumping all around. Some of the girls were there, and about a half hour later the first TV station came to interview Red. It was a great day for our entire family.

— Mary Schoendienst

I joked at the time that anytime you can get a woman to not go shopping, that was big news.

There are people who are critical of the Veterans Committee and say it's not necessary anymore, but I don't agree with them. Those guys are all voting on players that they saw play, and are able to recognize which ones deserve to be in the Hall of Fame. A perfect case in point is former Phillies' outfielder Richie Ashburn, who unfortunately passed away last summer. All you had to do to understand that he was deserving was look at his record, but for some reason he never was voted in by the writers. That mistake was rectified by the Veterans Committee, fortunately while Richie was still alive. Richie was a great player. He played terrific in centerfield and always had a lot of assists and he was the leadoff hitter who got the Phillies going. When you played against Philadelphia in that era you thought of Ashburn before you thought of anyone else.

When you look at the ballot of players the writers have to choose from, sometimes I can see where they have tough choices to make. They let the writers vote for up to 10 people, but I think most only vote for three or four. You would like to think politics and whether a player cooperated with the media wouldn't enter into the decision on whether a player should be elected to the Hall of Fame, but you know it does. One simple rule you know is true is if you played in New York, you're going to get more votes. It's simple, because there are more writers from New York, especially in the earlier years when they had more newspapers. I played in New York, but I don't think my one year there ever garnered me any additional votes.

I don't think I was ever truly nervous before a baseball game, even the seventh game of the World Series, when I was playing. I have to admit I was nervous when I found out I had been elected to the Hall of Fame. Thinking about what the day would be like, and that I would have to give a speech in front of all the other great players in the crowd, made me break into a sweat. I enjoyed all the phone calls and congratulatory messages, but I knew the day I would have to stand up and make that speech would come pretty quickly.

Red was on the road coaching, and I kept saying we needed to get his speech going. Everybody wanted to put in their own two cents' worth, and all of the children had their own ideas of what they wanted Red to say. We typed up the speech, and when Red got home he had very little time to look at it. It was so hectic he went to the bathroom and finally read it there. He came out and said it was a good speech, but he wasn't sure he could do it. We all offered him a lot of encouragement, telling him he could do it, and hollered at him until he had all of the words pronounced correctly.

— Mary Schoendienst

The induction ceremony is on Sunday, but we all flew to Cooperstown on Thursday. They really have a lot of activities for all of the Hall of Famers over the entire weekend, and the small New York village becomes the center of the baseball world for those three days. You walk down the main street and you can run into some of the most famous people in the history of the game. You see fans who attend every year, and you see people who come especially to see somebody they admired as a player be inducted into the Hall. We had a lot of people there to honor me, including several busloads from Germantown. That helped make the weekend even more special.

On Friday there is a big party for all of the Hall of Famers, and on Saturday they have a charity scramble golf tournament. On Sunday before the ceremony they open the golf course just for the Hall of Famers, and it really is a nice day. Getting together with all of the players you played with and against brings back a lot of happy memories. I know for a lot of former players, that weekend is the highlight of their summer.

As the day of the ceremony approached, I got even more nervous. Part of the reason I was a little apprehensive was I've never been fond of talking in front of a large audience, and since I had never been to the induction ceremonies, I was a little unsure about what exactly was going to transpire.

Johnny Bench and Carl Yastrzemski were being inducted as well, having been voted in by the writers, and all of us were staying in a building waiting for the ceremony to begin. It was a very hot day, and the air conditioning in the building went out. We were all sweating, and that probably contributed to making me even more nervous.

I had played with and against Warren Spahn, and he was one of the other Hall of Famers there that day. Just as I was getting ready to be introduced and walk out onto the stage, the always-joking Spahn said to me, "Don't mess up now." He'd given me something else to think about.

Mary was worried that I might break down and cry. That happens to a lot of guys, but that was one thing I honestly never thought would happen. A German would not cry. A lot of people become emotional because they realize what this moment means. It is the ultimate. You play for years and years, you have individual success and team success, you go through big games and the World Series games, and you realize this is the last stage of your career. Everybody who gets to the Hall of Fame has to realize they have been very fortunate in this game, and realize that so many players never get to experience this honor. It's like playing in the World Series in that a lot of players play for years and years and never make it. I knew I was a pretty fortunate guy.

It came time for me to give my speech, and I was more nervous than I had been before any game in my career. I knew I could play better than I could speak, but I didn't have that option now. I had to talk.

My speech focused on how lucky I had been, and how many great memories I had of playing the game for 19 years. I mentioned all of the great players I had played with, against or managed, which I think stacks up favorably with anybody else. I also talked about my old roommate, Musial.

"My best memories are of being a Cardinal, and I'm glad Stan and I will be roommates once again—here in the Hall of Fame," I said.

Colleen had an idea and she talked about it with Uncle Joe (Linneman) that everybody in our group would wear red Orphan Annie wigs to the ceremony. It was so hot that day but everybody wore those wigs. Joe also had got everybody a red windbreaker with No. 2 and Schoendienst printed on it. People were coming up to us and wanting to buy them. Those wigs were so hot they made everybody perspire, but we wore them, even while we were walking around in town. Everybody there had a great time.
— Mary Schoendienst

A tradition at the Hall of Fame is that on Sunday night following the induction ceremony, they have a dinner exclusively for the Hall of Famers. Wives or children or friends can't come. It's a very exclusive group. We knew that was going to be going on Sunday night, so Joe Linneman arranged to rent out a big room in one of the restaurants in Cooperstown and he treated everybody in our party—I think it was more than 125 people—to dinner. Whoever was around he invited to dinner, including Lil Musial and Isabelle Medwick. He wanted to make certain everybody besides me and Stan had a good time, and they did. It was nice of him to do that, and it was something he didn't have to do.

When you are involved in the ceremony, you don't really get much time to enjoy the weekend and all of the festivities. They have another tradition of all of the Hall of Famers signing autographs for kids. Every Hall of Famer has his own postcard, with a picture of his plaque, and that's what he signs. The kids line up and you sign for two or three hours. It's days like that I sometimes wish my last name was Smith or Jones instead of Schoendienst. Your hand can get a little tired after a while.

I didn't get to go into the Hall and look at all of the exhibits and displays when I was there for the induction ceremony, but I have taken the time to do it when I have gone back. I have gone back every year since I was inducted and always enjoy getting together with all of the guys. People like Yogi Berra and Whitey Ford are there every year, and Spahn is usually there, although he missed the weekend in 1997.

When you walk in the main entrance, the first thing you see are statues of Babe Ruth and Ted Williams. That's pretty impressive to begin with. If you really want to take your time and look at everything, you had better plan on spending the majority of the day there. My brother Andy was there when I was inducted, and he didn't think he had enough time to look at everything. He said he wanted to come back when he had more time to really go through the Hall and museum and he and his friends did that, going back in the fall when there weren't as many people and the fall foliage really made it a pretty place.

People who have been to the other Halls of Fame for football, basketball and hockey always say that baseball is the best, but I can't make that statement because I haven't been to those places. All I know is the baseball hall would be pretty tough to beat.

The only other Hall of Fame to which I have been inducted is the Missouri Sports Hall of Fame in Springfield. They have built a nice place as well, and I try to go every January when the new class is inducted. The people there do a nice job and make it a real fun event.

It's always fun to see which players get elected to the Hall of Fame each year, by the writers and by the Veterans Committee, and I suppose I'm like everybody else in trying to determine if the guy deserves to be there. It's harder to do that for the people inducted into the Missouri Hall of Fame, because there players come from all sports.

In baseball, I like to think I'm a pretty fair judge of a player's ability and his character, but I'm glad I don't have to make the choice on whether to vote for or against any particular player. The one ingredient I look for in making a determination on a player, however, is whether he was consistent during his career. I don't think a player can make the Hall of Fame strictly as a reward for one terrific season. Some people think Roger Maris' record for most homers in a season should be enough for him to make the Hall of Fame but the voters who have judged him on his total career have decided other-wise. He had a good career, but never approached that level of hom-ers again.

Kenny Boyer is a guy who I think should be in the Hall. He was a consistent player, and he put up some very good numbers, but there probably are a lot of other guys who could make just as good a case as Kenny and they aren't in the Hall either. That shows you how exclusive the company is in the Hall of Fame.

There's been a big debate recently on whether Pete Rose should be in the Hall of Fame. The only comment I will make is that he knew the rules. They are displayed in every clubhouse and some-body reads them to all of the players every spring. A player is voted into the Hall of Fame for more than his playing ability, and I think that's the way it should be. A player's character and his integrity should have a bearing on whether or not he is elected. Most of the game's best players have no problems in those areas. They are just as good of citizens off the field as they are players on the field, and that's the kind of people you want in the Hall of Fame.

After you make your speech, there is a big feeling of relief. I might have choked up a little bit, but I didn't cry. Every year when I go back for the ceremonies, I can empathize with the new induct-ees because I know exactly what they are going through.

Going back to the Hall every year gives you a special feeling, because it's one weekend where all of the game's troubles are for-gotten and only the good times are remembered. When I look at all of the exhibits, and see things like the glove I used to set a fielding record for consecutive games without an error, it brings a smile to my face.

It was funny how that record ended. We were playing at the Polo Grounds, and there was a hit to the outfield. I went out to get the relay, and threw to third. The ball hit the runner sliding into the base, and went into the dugout. They awarded the runner home, and charged me with an error.

Another error I'll never forget came when I was playing with the Giants in a game against the Cardinals. Musial was batting, and he hit a sharp line drive that I fielded on one hop. It was hit so hard that it tore the webbing out of my glove. That kept me from getting another streak of errorless games going.

The people who run the Hall of Fame have asked for some other mementoes, and we have sent them a uniform. That seems appropriate since I have worn it for so many years.

I thought the Hall of Fame honor was going to be the final highlight of my career, but I was wrong. There was another day left, when the Cardinals announced they were going to retire my jersey number 2.

There are only a handful of players who have had that honor— Stan Musial with number 6, Enos Slaughter with number 9, Ken Boyer with number 14, Dizzy Dean with number 17, Lou Brock with number 20, Bob Gibson with number 45 and Ozzie Smith with number 1. To be one of only eight players among the hundreds who have played for the Cardinals who was recognized by having their jersey retired was truly a special honor.

Two other numbers are retired, but for different reasons. Gussie Busch was honored with a retired number, 85, for all of his contributions to the team and Jackie Robinson's number 42 was retired by all teams in 1997 as part of the 50th anniversary of his breaking the color barrier in 1947.

All of those honors and accolades might have caused some people to go into retirement and look back on their lives. Not me. I still had a uniform with my name and number on it and another game on the schedule. I was still looking ahead, not backward.

Chapter 13

COACHING BEATS WORKING

O ne of the best parts of my job and about having spent so much time in a Cardinal uniform is the opportunity to remain connected with a lot of the guys who played for me, including two who became my bosses, Joe Torre and Dal Maxvill.

A third, Mike Shannon, has had a long run in the broadcast booth with Jack Buck, and we became good golfing buddies on the road.

Being around people like Torre, Maxvill and Shannon kept my job fun and made coming to the ballpark an easy and enjoyable task. The hardest thing in life must be having to work at a job you don't like or enjoy or working with people you don't like. I know I'm lucky that never happened to me.

Torre didn't get many breaks during his tenure as the Cardinals' manager, but I thought he did a great job. It's unfortunate that the only way a manager's performance is really measured is by whether he wins or loses. People look at the record, but often times they don't look further to see the other factors that made that record either good or bad. A lot of times a team may finish .500, but the manager has done a terrific job and that record is simply an accurate reflection of the players' talent and abilities.

A lot of the good managers, like Whitey and Jim Leyland and Sparky Anderson, were very quick to admit they had good teams and good records because they had good players. Torre was and is a good manager—his championship with the Yankees in 1996 proved that.

When he was in St. Louis, there were a lot of moves Joe would have liked to have made that didn't go through. He couldn't get the players he wanted on his team, and we didn't win because of it.

One of the ways I judge a manager is by what his players think of him, and Joe was great in that area. He got along great with all his players, and that's what a manager is supposed to do. He was always talking with everybody, making certain he knew what was going on in their lives, and he cared about them as people and as players.

Joe was very good about not criticizing his players in public, and I know there were times he was extremely frustrated but he never let it show. If he had a problem with a particular player, he brought him in and they discussed the situation in private without anybody else from the team or the media knowing what that discussion was all about. That's the way it should be handled.

Joe had the advantage of being good personal friends with his boss, Maxvill, the general manager. It was the same kind of relationship I had with Stan when he was GM in 1967, and later with Bing as GM. Joe and Dal worked well together, but Dal was limited by what the executives at the brewery allowed him to do.

Dal knew baseball, and I think he had an idea about some trades that might have improved the ballclub, but he wasn't allowed to make them, primarily because of money. I know in spring training Dal would be sitting in the stands watching a game and a scout for another club would come up to discuss a possible deal. The first thing Dal would ask the scout was "how much is he making?" If the answer was above a certain amount, Dal said, "Forget it. We won't be able to do it."

That makes it tough, and it is part of the reason the GM's job is now the hardest job in baseball. A guy can know baseball, like Dal, and be a good evaluator of talent, but if he has budget constraints he just has to work that much harder to do his job.

The increase in salaries has had a bigger impact on the game in the last 20 years than anything else because it has impacted everything else. It's no coincidence that the teams that make the playoffs every year are almost always the ones that have the highest payrolls. That is a bad trend for baseball, but unfortunately I don't foresee the problem changing any time soon.

The changing economics of the game led to two developments in the mid 1990s—the player's strike in 1994 that wiped out much of the season and the World Series—and Anheuser-Busch's decision to sell the Cardinals prior to the 1996 season.

The strike, and the fact it lasted as long as it did and forced the cancelation of the playoffs and World Series, surprised me more than Busch's decision to sell the team. Not even a World War could stop the World Series, but the strike did. That was a real black eye for baseball, and it is something the game is still trying to overcome.

Anheuser-Busch's business is selling beer, and they do a better job of that than anybody else in the world. The Cardinals were just a small entry on the annual report, and I think the executives just decided it wasn't worth all of the problems and aggravation that the strike, rising salaries and so on was causing.

I do give the Anheuser-Busch executives credit for deciding to sell the team to some local owners who are great fans. It would have been very easy to simply look for the most money they could get and not care about the new owners, but they didn't do that. They picked guys who were committed to developing the ballclub and trying to put a winning team on the field.

Dal wasn't around to benefit from the new owners deciding to spend more money. He was fired, which surprised me, and was replaced by Walt Jocketty, who had a long career with Oakland and Colorado and was ready to move up to a GM's job.

Torre stayed on as manager when Jocketty took over, but he was in a tough position because he didn't know Walt and Walt didn't know him. When the team didn't perform as well as Walt had hoped, Torre was fired—the usual result of a poor performance. Walt didn't enjoy doing it, I know, but he thought it was a move that had to be made. When he drove out to Joe's house to tell him, Joe ended up consoling him more than the other way around. Joe even gave Walt a bottle of wine before he left. Walt was one of those pulling for Joe and the Yankees in 1996 and was very glad when they won and Joe got his World Series ring.

After Torre was fired, my former player list was down to one, Shannon, and we had some great times together. There isn't a town in the league where Shannon doesn't know somebody at a golf course, and he was always setting us up for an early-morning tee time, and off we went. The only place he didn't golf was New York, because there he wanted to go to the race track.

As many people as Shannon knows, he never got me on the course at Augusta, where the Masters is played. I really would like to play there someday. I'm not a good golfer, but I have fun and I don't get mad. That's my secret.

Every time a manager gets fired, people talk about how long he was there and it seems anymore it's only a couple of years, unless the team has won. As more time passes by, it becomes more amazing to me that I managed the Cardinals for 12 years. I was pretty fortunate to stay that long.

Managing today is not any harder than it was when I managed, but I don't think managers today want to stay on the job that long. They are making a lot more money today than managers made in my day, so they don't need to stay around that long. It will be pretty rare for a manager to stay around for 12 years in the future, especially with the same team.

Because of his many years in Oakland, the guy Jocketty wanted to replace Torre as manager was Tony La Russa. Walt did a good job to sell him on the job, and La Russa was hired before the 1996 season.

It took Tony a little while to adjust from the American League, because there is a difference in managing between the two leagues. The designated hitter rule changes the way the game is played, and makes a manager react differently to changing pitchers and using pinch-hitters. A manager makes more moves in the NL and has to always be thinking an inning or two ahead.

One thing about Tony that became apparent to me very quickly was his intensity. He's at the ballpark early every day and he stays late, even in spring training. He takes his job very seriously, and he works hard at it. Everybody has a different makeup, and that's just the way he approaches his job. It's a very consuming thing to him. I couldn't manage that way. I might have been intense for a very short period of time, but if I was that intense all the time I would be gone. Being that intense all the time would just wear me down mentally as well as physically.

Tony seems to be able to handle it, however, and shows no signs of wearing down. He was frustrated the team didn't perform better in 1997, after everybody thought we had a good chance to repeat as division champions, but it didn't work out that way. Sometimes those things happen.

Tony is a good baseball man. He understands the game, and he keeps the club disciplined. He has the respect of the players, and he communicates well with them. Because he and Walt have that good manager-GM relationship, they are able to work well together and Walt has been able to make the moves and get the players that Tony thought would improve the ballclub.

One of the beauties of my job is I never have to interfere or get involved in making decisions unless Tony or Walt asks me for an opinion. Tony takes the responsibility, and never backs away from a challenge. He's like any other good manager—if he has the players, he's going to win. It's hard to do it every year, but I like the Cardinals' chances in 1998 if everybody stays healthy.

Being around the ballclub still is a very enjoyable experience for me. I usually am on the field during batting practice, hitting fungoes and just talking with guys around the cage behind home plate. You see a lot of people there that you know from other clubs, writers and broadcasters, and you have time to chat with them about what's going on in their lives.

Players today are different, there's no doubt about it, but that doesn't make them bad guys. The money involved in the game today has changed the players, and made baseball much more of a business than a game. Still, the majority of players realize how fortunate they are and are fun guys to be around. These guys would benefit more if they had spent more time in the minor leagues, learning the fundamentals and having to ride buses and suffer a little financially, to really appreciate being in the major leagues.

There are some great ballplayers in the major leagues today, but I don't think it's fair to compare players from different eras. The game was played differently, the ball was different, the parks were different, the travel was different, the equipment was different— too many variables to say this current guy is a better player than a guy from the 1930s or 1940s. During the 1996 season, some people were trying to say the outfield of Ron Gant, Ray Lankford and Brian Jordan was as good as the 1942 outfield of Stan Musial, Terry Moore and Enos Slaughter, and I don't see how you can say that.

The simple way to look at comparing players from different generations is that the great players from another era would be great players today and the great players today would have been just as great had they been playing 30 or 40 years ago. Anyone who wants to take it any further than that is fighting a losing battle.

Expansion and the lack of pitching depth has weakened the level of talent in the game, I believe, but it's still at a competitive level and that's the most important thing. I've never seen a bad ballgame. You see a few things you may not be satisfied with, but as long as the players go out there and hustle and play hard, the fans have to believe they are getting their money's worth.

Fans in St. Louis are different from fans in a lot of cities, especially places like Philadelphia, New York and Boston. They want the Cardinals to win, but they mainly want to see players hustle and give 100 percent. If they do that and lose, they are not going to be too upset. When fans here get down on a player, you know he must have really done something terrible.

What has amazed me the last couple of years is the way the fans react to Willie McGee. He may be the most popular player to ever play for the Cardinals. I'm talking about popular, not the best player, even though he is very good. Every time he walks up to the plate to hit, he gets a standing ovation. When he came back to the Cardinals after being on other teams for a couple of years, it was like a hero had come back to town.

The people respond to him for a couple of reasons—the way he plays on the field, and the fact he never says anything controversial or critical about another player or manager. You never see him lay back, he always is giving everything he's got, running ground balls out hard every time. Everything he does on the field he does hard.

Everybody remembers the game he had in Milwaukee in the 1982 World Series, and that might have been one of the greatest individual performances in the history of the World Series. He should have been the MVP of that series. He has won the MVP in the league, in 1985, and it was well deserved. Willie just knows how to play the game, and he's a winner.

Ozzie Smith really took Willie under his wing and helped him mature during the early 1980s, both as a player and a person, and it's nice now to see some of the younger players on the team coming up to Willie for advice and suggestions, which Willie always gives to them. He has become a real leader in the clubhouse.

Even though Willie's popularity has been long lasting, I don't think I've ever seen a player join a team and take over a town the way Mark McGwire did when he hit St. Louis in August and September of 1997. It was unbelievable. Every time he came to the plate or his name was announced, he got a standing ovation. He usually came through with a home run as well.

People look at his final total of 58 homers and talk about what a great year it was—and it was—but they forget that he struggled for the first couple of weeks after the trade from Oakland. If he had just snuck in another homer or two during that stretch he could have been right there with Ruth and Maris' mark going into the final days of the season. Then the fans really would have had something to cheer about.

I've seen a lot of guys hit baseballs a long way, but there's something different about the way McGwire hits them. He hits them high in addition to hitting them far. The ball could very well be wound tighter than it used to be, but McGwire's power has nothing to do with the ball.

Having him on the team for a full season should be really entertaining for the fans and hopefully will be the key to getting the Cardinals back in the playoffs again.

The 1998 season will mark the 54th consecutive season I've worn a major-league uniform and the 49th year wearing a Cardinals' uniform. That's a long time, but it doesn't feel like it's been that long. It's still a joy to put that uniform on every day and I'm going to keep doing it for as long as I can.

Baseball was a great game before I began to play it, it was a great game when I played it and managed, and it's still a great game. It always will be, no matter how much some people try to mess it up. As long as they don't change the distance of the pitching mound and the bases, you can't totally mess it up.

What makes baseball so great is you can't hold the ball for 24 seconds and take the last shot or run the clock down and kick a field goal. You have to get 27 outs, one way or the other. Time doesn't run out until you get that 27th out.

Everything I have in my life I owe to baseball. I've been lucky in so many ways, making a career out of something I loved to do as a kid. It's been a great ride, and I'm not ready to end it yet.

Chapter 14

A GREAT RIDE

When Pop came down from painting that bridge to sign my first professional contract, all he asked the Cardinals' scouts was to give me a chance, and that's all they promised. He didn't know what would happen to me; I didn't, and neither did the scouts.

Pop worked his whole life, either as a coal miner, an electrician, a carpenter and as a state prison guard. He always was doing something. He even found a job during the Depression, and that was hard to do. If he were alive today, he wouldn't believe how much the world has changed.

They didn't have highways when I was a kid, and most people never left the town they were born in. Some people in Germantown stayed their entire lives. It was hard to find a radio to listen to the ballgame, and then came television and everything else. I don't know where the technology improvements are going to stop.

I can't imagine having lived in a more exciting period of history, to have experienced all of the events that have occurred in the last 70 years. I've been extremely fortunate, and I'm not afraid to say it.

If there is one place I feel just as at home as a ballpark, it's out in a field, hunting for quail or ducks. Ever since I was a little kid, hunting has been a constant for me. It's my therapy, it's where I go to think about things and work out my problems.

I love to be out there watching the dogs work. When you've got good dogs, watching them work is like watching a great ballplayer. I like being out in the action, walking, being away from telephones and enjoying the challenge. It's another game to me, and one I thoroughly enjoy.

I'm up and gone before most people get up in the morning, and by the time the sun comes up I'm out in the field, listening to the birds, ready for the day. I go quail hunting, duck hunting and goose hunting. I don't hunt for deer because there's not enough action for me. You have to sit in one place too long.

You have time to think when you're hunting, and you're doing it in the fresh air and with a clear mind. Fishing is the same way. Sitting in a boat, watching the birds, enjoying the calm and peace and quiet. That's pretty hard to beat.

I've done pretty much what I wanted to do my whole life, and I know not a lot of people are lucky enough to be able to say that. That's part of the reason I appreciate everything that has happened to me, because I know how lucky I am. What kid doesn't dream of playing in the World Series, or sharing the field with some of the greatest players ever to play baseball? What kid doesn't dream of becoming friends with a lot of famous people, and of being inducted into the Hall of Fame? Baseball has been so good to me and my family.

A lot of people would not want to be around the game as long as I have, but I can't imagine doing anything else. I was fortunate the Cardinals still wanted me around. I knew baseball better than anything else, so I stayed with it. I really don't know how much longer I'll stay around, but I enjoy what I'm doing now and want to keep at it as long as I am physically able.

It upsets me when people criticize the game of baseball and take shots at it, because the game is not the problem. There were great players before I came along like Babe Ruth and Dizzy Dean,

there were great players when I played, there are great players playing today and there will be great players playing in the future. The
owners have got to get together with the players and figure out
how to fix the problems, and how to make the game even better.

They have got to figure out a way to get more of a balance in
the game. The Players' Association runs the game today, and it
shouldn't be that way. Baseball needs a commissioner who understands both sides of the game. It's the greatest game going, but it
needs direction.

Games are too long, and it's because the umpires don't force
the hitters to get up there and hit and stop messing around. Umpires also need to call the strike zone the way the rule book reads.
Now any pitch above the belt is a ball, and that's not where the
strike zone is supposed to stop. Kids today who throw hard are
going to run that ball up there and it's tough to hit. It should be
called a strike, but most of the time if the batter doesn't swing it's a
ball. That makes the game longer, too.

Baseball has more competition today than when I was a kid.
Kids are playing football, basketball, hockey and soccer and partici-
pating in other sports like golf and tennis. There has got to be a way
to get kids back to playing baseball, but I don't know what it is.

There's competition not only from other sports, but from computer games and Nintendo and television shows. Part of the reason
you see so many Latin players in the major leagues is the kids in
those countries were like the kids of my generation—we didn't have
all of those choices. If we were looking for something to do, we
went outside and played baseball.

One of the standard arguments why baseball doesn't attract
more kids is that you have to have a group of kids to play, but I don't
agree with it. A kid can take a basketball and go out by himself and
shoot, but I also used to take a baseball or a tennis ball and throw it
up against the side of the house and play catch with myself as a kid
when I had nobody else to play with. It can be done.

The biggest problem with all kids sports today is that everything has to be too organized. You very seldom see a group of kids
playing by themselves in a vacant lot, and that's a shame. Of course
there aren't as many vacant lots around anymore either. Almost

every kid plays on a team in an organized league and he's either playing in a game or at an organized practice or not at all.

The other "problem" with baseball from a kid's viewpoint, at least from what I've heard and read, is that the game is boring. There's no up-and-down action like basketball and hockey, and that might be true to a certain extent. You have to look for something different in baseball, and if you look, you can find it. You see something different every game.

Baseball isn't a game that lends itself well to television, like basketball, because of the pace of the game. You have to really want to follow the game and be involved not to have your mind wander a little when watching a game on television. Kids have trouble doing that, which is why they prefer to watch basketball.

It's different when you actually come to the stadium to watch a game, no matter if it's the majors or the minors. There is action going on, it just can't be shown on television where the camera is almost always focused on the pitcher or the batter. There's other stuff to see, but you have to be at the ballpark to see it.

There are a lot smarter people than me working in the marketing departments of all the baseball teams, and they know the problems of the game just as well as I do. They are working hard to come up with programs and plans to try to make the game more attractive to kids, and I think it will happen.

There has been some talk of altering the rules in the future to spark new interest in the game, like cutting it down to three balls for a walk and two strikes for an out. That won't happen. You can have the designated hitter and interleague play and the wild card and even a team changing leagues like Milwaukee, but doing something radical like that would be a huge mistake. There are too many loyal fans who love the game the way it is despite all of its problems, and a move like that would force even them to find something else to do with their time and money.

I try not to look too far into the future, because I'm having so much fun in the present. There are things I would like to do in my life, and I hope I get the opportunity to do them.

I would love to play golf on the Masters course at Augusta, and I would love to go to the Kentucky Derby. I've been lucky to have spent so much time around celebrities and famous people from all walks of life, and I know that I've been fortunate. I've played golf with Arnold Palmer and Gary Player, and that was a big thrill.

I've been to Palmer's house in Latrobe, Pennsylvania, and watched how he makes his own clubs. That's something a lot of people don't get to do. I like to watch the young guys play as well. It's amazing how well they can hit the ball and what they can make it do with their clubs.

I've had my picture taken with Helen Hayes, the first lady of the theater. That was a thrill. I wish I would have had my picture taken with Jackie Gleason, but I never did. We watched the "Bonanza" television show being shot in Los Angeles, and that was a neat experience.

We went back stage on the Broadway shows to meet some of the stars and the big band leaders. Those guys were great baseball fans. I never got to meet Glenn Miller or Spencer Tracy, and I wish I had the chance to do that. Tracy was one of my favorite actors.

Unlike a lot of players, I did spend a lot of time with my family during my career and I always was grateful for that. I want to spend more time with Mary and all of my children, my three daughters and son Kevin, in the future. Mary has been with me through almost everything in my life, and we have so much to be thankful for. She has a great singing voice, and it always was great listening to her sing. Our daughter Colleen sings a lot now and does a great job. Mary suffered a stroke a couple of years ago, but thankfully has recovered quite well. As I learned when I was suffering from tuberculosis, your health is the most important thing in the world, and anybody who takes it for granted is making a big mistake.

As I have gotten older, I have truly enjoyed my grandkids. We have 10; a full baseball team plus a relief pitcher.

Our oldest daughter, Colleen, is married to Hank Schwetye and they have two boys and a girl: Henry, Erin and James. The funny thing was after Erin was born, we didn't realize that we suddenly had Henry Erin in our family. Henry is an outstanding lacrosse player in high school and he and James like to go golfing with me any chance they get. Erin plays soccer and is terrific. She has been named to several All-America teams and likely will earn a college scholarship to play soccer.

Mary was very proud when Colleen and Hank decided to name their third child James, after Mary's dad. He plays baseball too, and will be playing second base for his grade school team this year.

Our second daughter, Cathleen, is married to Mark Reifsteck and they have three sons: Karl, Peter and Michael. Karl, the oldest at 16, enjoys sports but also excels academically. He plays soccer and baseball and wrestles, and is proud to represent his high school, St. Louis Priory. His kindness and generosity to others is outstanding. He is always willing to help with a patient smile.

Peter is next and is a very interesting child. Three months after his birth, we received some shocking news. After numerous medical tests, it was discovered that he has a rare retina condition. Peter is legally blind but uses every bit of vision he has. Now 13, Peter reads and writes using Braille and is a very active teenager. He attends his local school in Kirkwood and makes the honor roll.

Mary loves to hear Peter play the piano, especially Beethoven's Fifth and The Entertainer from The Sting. He has a quick wit and loves the outdoors. We are proud of his accomplishments and I still marvel that he rides a bike and participates in downhill skiing. In fact, upon returning from Colorado recently, his father remarked that he can no longer guide Peter as Peter skis so fast he is right on Mark's skis at the finish of the run.

Cathleen's third son, Michael, is also legally blind. He is a busy toddler, 16 months old, and always in a hurry. Sometimes he looks as if he is stealing bases as he runs from the kitchen to the living room, around the corner to the family room and back. He loves to play with me and he flirts and charms everyone he meets. He adores his big brothers and is always ready to play a game or read a book.

Eileen and her husband John Schless have two children, Mary and Patrick. They used to live in New Hampshire, and made several trips to Cooperstown to visit the Hall of Fame. Patrick was only six weeks old when I was inducted, and a couple of years later when his family was there, he said, "someday I'm going to be here with my grandpa." We got to make that trip, and it was fun for both of us.

Both Mary and Patrick are good kids as well as good athletes. Patrick plays baseball every chance he gets, but discovered basketball this year and realized there are other sports. Mary takes more of an intellectual and analytical approach to sports, but seems to have found a niche playing volleyball. Both Mary and Patrick are good tennis players, just like their mom and dad. Like all our grandchildren, they have always tried to do their best and have fun at whatever they were doing.

Kevin has two daughters, Jennifer and Kendall. As a freshman in high school, Jennifer won the Florida state championship for the two-mile cross country run. She probably would have won more titles, but has spent the last two years trying to recover from torn ligaments in her ankle. Kendall is a good soccer player and is one of the few girls on a boy-dominated team. She likes the challenge of beating them.

It's fun to get them all together and see the differences in their personalities. They are all good children, and Mary and I are proud of each of them; just as we are proud of all of our own children. It's really a treat when they visit.

It's tough for a lot of ballplayers to enjoy their families and spend time with them. People look at all the money they make and think they have a great and easy life, but so many of them live and work in different cities than their families, and that forces them to go long periods without seeing each other. That's a tough thing to do, no matter how much money you make. I was lucky I spent so many years playing, managing and coaching in St. Louis that I got to be with my family. I got to watch my children grow up, and enjoyed their special moments.

It was easier both for me and for Mary and the children that we didn't have to move around all over the country. They got to stay home, be with their friends, and enjoy the kind of childhood a child is supposed to have.

Mary and I celebrated our 50th wedding anniversary in September 1997, and we had a big party. All of the kids and family and close friends came, and it was a special night. Everybody was kidding us that we really hadn't been married 50 years because I was gone half the time, and maybe that was the secret to our marriage.

Actually, the secret was that I married a great lady who did a terrific job taking care of the house and raising the kids. I was lucky, and I know that.

All four of our children are special to me as well. Cathleen and Colleen still live in St. Louis so we see them and their families quite often. Eileen lives in Kansas City, not too far away, and Kevin is in Jacksonville, Florida.

Our family always gets together either at Thanksgiving or at Christmas, and everybody has a great time together. It's during those occasions that somebody my age reflects on their life, and how it has turned out, and I honestly don't know how my life could have been any better.

I did everything I wanted to do. I played baseball and have spent the rest of my life working in the game. I married a wonderful woman and she helped me raise four great kids. Now we are helping our kids with their kids, and that's what life is supposed to be about.

You always would have liked to have done more. There always are regrets in anybody's life about missed opportunities or one more goal they would have liked to have reached. I would have liked to have led the National League in hitting, but it didn't happen. I came close, but fell a couple of hits shy. I don't waste much time lamenting that disappointment. I have far too many other things to be happy and rejoice about.

Before every ballgame, the Star Spangled Banner is played. Hearing that song still gives me a warm feeling. I wouldn't have been able to lead the life I've led in any other country in the world. Kate Smith used to sing "God Bless America" and it always thrilled me. It made me hesitate, appreciating all the blessings I had received.

It wasn't too far into my playing career when Bob Broeg hung a nickname on me—Huck Finn. He thought I was the personification of the famous Mark Twain character, and I guess in a lot of ways that's true. I've read *Huckleberry Finn* and *Tom Sawyer*, and I think those books taught me one lesson—life is what you make it. Try to make the best of it.

In the minor leagues when I didn't have money, I tried to sleep late so I wouldn't have to eat. I knew what I wanted to achieve in my life, and I did it through baseball. I put every ounce I had into it, and the ride has been terrific. I really have no regrets. The horse hasn't kicked me off yet, but it's a little tamer now.

I'm blessed, very blessed.

Schoendienst's Stats

Albert Fred "Red" Schoendienst
Born February 2, 1923, Germantown, Illinois
Hall of Fame, 1989

Year	Team, League		G	W	L	T	N	PCT	Standing		
1965	STL	N	162	80	81	1	0	.497	7		
1966			162	83	79	0	0	.512	6		
1967			161	101	60	0	0	.627	1		
1968			162	97	65	0	0	.599	1		
1969			162	87	75	0	0	.537	4		
1970			162	76	86	0	0	.469	4		
1971			163	90	72	1	0	.556	2		
1972			156	75	81	0	0	.481	4		
1973			162	81	81	0	0	.500	2		
1974			161	86	75	0	0	.534	2		
1975			163	82	80	1	0	.506	3		
1976			162	72	90	0	0	.444	5		
1980			37	18	19	0	0	.486	5	4	
1990			24	13	11	0	0	.542	6	6	6
	14 yrs.		1999	1041	955	3	0	.522			

World Series

Year	Team, League		G	W	L	T	N	PCT
1967	STL	N	7	4	3	0	0	.571
1968			7	3	4	0	0	.429
	2 yrs.		14	7	7	0	0	.500

Year	Club	League	Pos.	G.	AB.	R.	H.	2B.	3B.	HR.	RBI.	B.A.	PO.	A.	E.	F.A.
1942	Union City	Kitty	2B	6	27	4	11	3	0	0	4	.407	16	20	2	.947
1942	Albany	Ga.-Fla.	S-2B	68	264	41	71	7	5	1	28	.269	155	209	27	.931
1943	Lynchburg	Pied.	SS	9	36	8	17	2	0	0	5	.472	18	36	3	.947
1943	Rochester	Int.	SS	136	555	81	*187	21	5	6	37	*.337	*339	*438	48	.942
1944	Rochester †	Int.	SS	25	102	26	38	3	2	2	14	.373	50	84	17	.887
1945	St. Louis	Nat.	OF-S-2	137	565	89	157	22	6	1	47	.278	302	30	10	.971
1946	St. Louis	Nat.	*2-3-SS	142	606	94	170	28	5	0	34	.281	363	379	13	*.983
1947	St. Louis	Nat.	2-3-OF	151	*659	91	167	25	9	3	48	.253	364	417	19	.976
1948	St. Louis	Nat.	2B	119	408	64	111	21	4	4	36	.272	230	269	10	.980
1949	St. Louis	Nat.	*2-S-3-O	151	640	102	190	25	2	3	54	.297	*428	*471	15	*.984
1950	St. Louis	Nat.	2-S-3	153	*642	81	177	*43	9	7	63	.276	425	437	14	.984
1951	St. Louis	Nat.	2B-SS	135	553	88	160	32	7	6	54	.289	354	419	10	.987
1952	St. Louis	Nat.	*2-3-SS	152	620	91	188	40	7	7	67	.303	*417	460	20	.978
1953	St. Louis	Nat.	2B	146	564	107	193	35	5	15	79	.342	*365	*430	14	*.983
1954	St. Louis	Nat.	2B	148	610	98	192	38	8	5	79	.315	394	*477	18	.980
1955	St. Louis	Nat.	2B	145	553	68	148	21	3	11	51	.268	296	381	10	*.985
1956	St. L.‡-N.Y.	Nat.	2B	132	487	61	147	21	8	2	29	.302	298	308	4	*.993
1957	N.Y.§-Milw.	Nat.	•2B-OF	150	648	91	*200	31	8	15	65	.309	379	448	12	•.986
1958	Milwaukee	Nat.	2B	106	427	47	112	23	1	1	24	.262	233	301	7*	.987
1959	Milwaukee x	Nat.	2B	5	3	0	0	0	0	0	0	.000	1	1	1	.667
1960	Milwaukee y	Nat.	2B	68	226	21	58	9	1	1	19	.257	120	148	10	.964
1961	St. Louis	Nat.	2B	72	120	9	36	9	0	1	12	.300	43	42	4	.955
1962	St. Louis	Nat.	2B-3B	98	143	21	43	4	0	2	12	.301	33	48	1	.988
1963	St. Louis	Nat.	PH	6	5	0	0	0	0	0	0	.000	0	0	0	.000
Major League Totals			2216	8479	1223	2449	427	78	84	773	.289	5045	5466	192	?	.982

† Entered Military Service in May.

‡ Traded to New York Giants with Pitchers Gordon Jones and Dick Littlefield, Catcher Bill Sarni and Outfielder Jack Brandt for Pitcher Don Liddle, Catcher Ray Katt, Shortstop Al Dark and Outfielder-First Baseman Whitey Lockman. All players but Jones exchanged clubs June 14, 1956—Jones being assigned to Giants, October 1, 1956.

§ Traded to Milwaukee Braves for Pitcher Ray Crone. Second Baseman Danny O'Connell and Outfielder Bobby Thomson, June 15, 1957.

x On disabled list with tuberculosis most of season.

y Released by Milwaukee Braves, October 14, 1960; signed by St. Louis Cardinals, March 15, 1961.

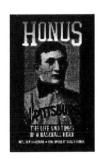

The Perfect Yankee ($22.95)

By all accounts, the no-hit, perfect game pitched by New York Yankee right-hander Don Larsen in the 1956 World Series qualifies as a true miracle. No one knows why it happened, or why an unlikely baseball player like Don Larsen was chosen to perform it. In *The Perfect Yankee,* Don Larsen and co-author Mark Shaw describe for the first time the facts surrounding one of the most famous games in baseball history. Autographed copies (with Larsen's signature) are available by calling Sports Publishing Inc. at 1-800-327-5557.

Lou Boudreau: Covering all the Bases ($24.95)

This is the personal story of one of the most extraordinary men in baseball history. While leading the Cleveland Indians to a World Series victory in 1948, he invented the "Ted Williams shift," and became the only player/manager ever to win the American League Most Valuable Player award. Boudreau with co-author Russell Schneider tells about winning the 1944 American League Batting Championship with a hit in his final at-bat of the season, and how he became the youngest manager in baseball history at the age of 24. His illustrious playing career culminated in 1970, when he was voted into the Baseball Hall of Fame. Autographed copies (Boudreau) are available by calling Sports Publishing Inc. at 1-800-327-5557.

Just Call Me Minnie ($19.95)

In *Just Call Me Minnie,* Saturnino Orestes Arrieta Armas Minoso tells his incredible story. The living drama of this six-decade baseball legend is told with help from author Herb Fagen with a rare blend of candor, insight, and honesty. Minnie says, "I want to finally open my heart. There are lots of thing I haven't been able to say until now." Autographed copies (Minoso) are available by calling Sports Publishing Inc. at 1-800-327-5557.

All titles are availables at your local bookstore or by calling Sports Publishing Inc. at 1-800-327-5557